The Obs⌐_ . ⌐_

Matt Charman's first play, *A Night at the Dogs*, won
the Verity Bargate Award and was performed at the
Soho Theatre in 2005. His second, *The Five Wives
of Maurice Pinder*, premiered at the National Theatre
in 2007. Matt was Pearson Writer in Residence at the
National Theatre throughout 2008. He is a recipient
of a Peggy Ramsay Award and a winner of the
Catherine Johnson Prize.

MATT CHARMAN

The Observer

ff

faber and faber

First published in 2009
by Faber and Faber Limited
74–77 Great Russell Street, London WC1B 3DA

Typeset by Country Setting, Kingsdown, Kent CT14 8ES
Printed in England by CPI Bookmarque, Croydon, Surrey

A CIP record for this book
is available from the British Library

978-0-571-24973-2

2 4 6 8 10 9 7 5 3 1

Acknowledgements

I owe an unpayable debt of gratitude to both Peter
Hatch and Elizabeth Freestone who were instrumental
in the development of this play at the National Theatre
Studio. I must also thank Tom Scutt and all of the
actors involved in the first workshops of the piece.
I am indebted too to Michael McCoy, Purni Morell,
Sebastian Born and Nicholas Hytner for an awful lot
of encouraging coffees and constructive notes. I'd also
like to thank Chidube Nri, Jude Akuwudike and
Reginald Ofodile for their amazing work on the Igbo
translations, and Anwen Hooson and James Westcott
for being my first (very) forgiving readers. Lastly,
Richard Eyre whose passion and laser-like focus has
been an education in playwriting like I've never known.

The **Observer** was first presented in the Cottesloe auditorium of the National Theatre, London, on 13 May 2009. The cast was as follows:

Fiona Russell Anna Chancellor
Daniel Okeke Chuk Iwuji
Saunders James Fleet
Declan Lloyd Hutchinson
Muturi / Mr Sesay Louis Mahoney
Edi / Judy Isabel Pollen
Obinna / Soldier / Security Man / Policeman Daon Broni
Fabian / Henrik Peter Forbes
Tony Leo Bill
Duduzile / Chimma / Receptionist Joy Richardson
Arya / Dr Daramy / The General / Wink Cyril Nri
Kalifa / Waletta / Chairwoman Aicha Kossoko

Director Richard Eyre
Designer Rob Howell
Lighting Designer Neil Austin
Music Richard Hartley
Sound Designer Rich Walsh
Igbo Language Coach Jude Akuwudike

Characters

in order of appearance

Saunders
Foreign Office civil servant

Fabian
Chief of the International Election Observation Team

Fiona Russell
Deputy Chief of the Observation Team

Daniel Okeke
student and Fiona's translator

Aarya
election observer

Kalifa
head of a polling station

Tony
member of the Observation Team

Edi
member of the Observation Team

Declan
BBC journalist

Henrik
replacement Chief of the Observation Team

Muturi
Daniel's father

Madam Conteh
Chair of the Electoral Committee

Mr Sesay
committee member

Dr Daramy
committee member

Stenographer

Policeman

Duduzile
a mother

Obinna
Duduzile's son

Wink
bar owner

Waletta
Wink's wife

Chimma
waitress

Judy
BBC camerawoman

Soldier

General Okute
senior member of the armed forces

The doubling or even tripling of certain parts
is possible, the intention being that the twenty-three
characters could be played by a company of twelve

THE OBSERVER

'Power does its work by stealth,
and the powerful can subsequently deny
that their strength was ever used at all.'

Salman Rushdie
Shalimar the Clown

Time and Setting

Present day. A country in West Africa

Language

English and Igbo

Staging

Scenes should move as fluidly as possible
with just a hint of the various locations stated.
Also, while the 'screen' mentioned in the stage
directions is used to display captions, specified
translated material and news footage, other
solutions might also be found to perform the
same function

Act One

ONE

Saunders, a man in a creased suit, faces us and speaks.

Saunders There's an expression in the Foreign Office.
'Bollocked off' – meaning, to be retired, semi-retired
or put out of harm's way. In a place like this. You
can put up a fight of course. I knew a chap who did.
Told them where to stick it, now he runs his own dried
flower business. But that's not really my scene. This is.
My scene, I mean. Running the odd errand for the
Embassy. Standing in at some second-rate ceremonial
engagement. And of course, watching. Sitting,
watching, waiting. For three years. For nothing.
Then she came.

TWO

*Fiona stands and watches as Fabian vomits into a
wastepaper basket. By his feet is a packed suitcase.
After a moment he straightens up, shivers and wipes
his mouth.*

Fabian I'm recommending that they don't give you
my job. I hope you don't take it the wrong way but
I'm recommending Henrik over you. My cab is on its

3

way. Thanks for coming in so early. I just didn't want it to be awkward in front of the team. Excuse me.

Fabian heaves again but isn't sick this time. Fiona stays watching him. He wipes his mouth out of habit. He looks frail and old as he clutches the bin close to him.

It's going to be murder on the plane . . . People have been suggesting I get one of those pens with the ultraviolet light that you stir your glass of water with to purify it. I must have had that advice a hundred times this week.

Fiona Sounds like a good idea.

Fabian This has got nothing to do with the water. I wonder how much weight I've lost. You can't be sick for an entire week and not lose a lot of weight, can you?

Fiona I wouldn't imagine.

Fabian What have people been saying?

Fiona About your weight?

Fabian About me leaving.

Fiona People don't want you to go, Fabian, but if you're not well . . .

Fabian I was sick in a jeep yesterday. We were driving out to do a recce of one of the government buildings, the one they're suggesting for the count in the capital. The huge one, the granite one.

Fiona I know it.

Fabian And I was sick, down myself. I felt so embarrassed. Are there bets on what's wrong with me?

When I was younger and my Head of Mission used to get sick, we always used to take bets on what it was. I rather hope there are bets.

Fiona There are bets.

Fabian Good.

He is nearly sick again but with deep breaths he manages to control it.

I've let things slide a bit. I'm sure you've noticed. We're behind schedule.

Fiona Only a little.

Fabian Not that it matters too much. The President is going to win, Fiona. The reason we're here is to observe a free and fair election and it'll be free and fair enough but the President is going to win.

Fiona I know.

Fabian So why am I recommending Henrik over you?

Fiona I don't know.

Fabian I want you to know . . . You've been a deputy for twelve years now. A damn good mission deputy for longer than anyone I know. Plus you've got three times more experience than him. You know your job and mine and everybody else's. So why am I recommending Henrik? I can't see through you, Fiona . . . I don't know what you're thinking. I never know.

Fiona stares back at him, without saying a word.

Right now is a perfect example.

Fiona And that's bad?

Fabian In this job, it's terrible. Look, you have to understand, I'm see-through. People look at me and they know exactly what they're going to get. Henrik is the same. You're different.

Fiona You're actually being serious, aren't you?

Fabian We all must be transparent. That is what we are. We are impartial, transparent, bores. I am. You know I am.

Fiona Yes, you are.

Fabian is offended by this.

Fabian Quite right. You see . . . and so is Henrik, almost as bad as me. He's a Labrador of a man. Simple, joyful, straightforward. You – you're something else entirely. You're interesting, Fiona.

Fiona Thank you.

Fabian Which is not to be trusted. He's going to win. The wrong man is going to win in the first round and we are going to record that it was free and fair enough and then we are going to go home.

Henrik will need a lot of help, of course. Look, I'm sorry, but I've made my decision . . . Please say something.

Fiona I'm proud of what I do, that's why I do it. And I've always done my job well. You've worked with me time and time again.

Fabian Because you're exceptional and I'm threatened by you and I love you.

Fiona looks at him thoroughly unimpressed.

Sorry. Try and remember I'm a little bit needy at the moment. I may not have meant that.

Fiona I've never given you cause to complain.

Fabian And I hope that you never will. I'm sorry, but my mind's made up. I'll see you back home in three weeks . . .
  It's pancreatic cancer, by the way. Who won the bet?

Fiona (*shocked, quietly*) Nobody.

Fabian Shame.

THREE

FOURTEEN DAYS UNTIL THE ELECTION:
LOCAL RECRUITMENT UNDER WAY

A young man with a rucksack on his back steps forward. He holds a single sheet of white paper in his hands. As he speaks this pledge in Igbo, his words appear translated into English on a screen behind him.

Daniel Aguala m we ghota ihe nile iwu kwuru maka ndi ana-akpo International Election Observers. [*I have read and understand the Code of Conduct for International Election Observers.*]
  Anoro m ebee nua iyi na odihu ihe mmeghe ma obu ihe mchoga ga anochi oru ayi gi'ru na ndoro ndoro ochichi. [*I hereby pledge that I have no conflicts of interest, political, economic nor other that will interfere with my ability to be an impartial election observer.*]
  Agaghim agbachi ndoro ndoro. [*I will not obstruct the election process.*]
  Agam asopuru iwu obodo na ike enyere ndi na

chikwata iso mpi a. [*I will respect national laws and the authority of election officials.*]

Agam eji ako na uchem we mara ihe nga-eme, were kwanu agwa oma mgbe obula ma mru ga oru ma mzuga ike. [*I will exercise sound judgement in personal interactions and observe the highest level of professional conduct at all times, including leisure time.*]

Agam ahu na eji ejiokwu mee ihe dum na iso mpi a, were dojie ahua oma International Election Observation Mission. [*I will protect the integrity of the International Election Observation Mission.*]

Agaghim agwa ndi na-ekwu okwu na ikuku ma obu ndi uwa ihe m choputara banyere ndoro ndoro nka – bere so ndi isi m Observation Mission's leadership, gwaram gwa ha. [*I will refrain from making personal comments, observations or conclusions to the news media or public before the Election Observation Mission makes a statement – unless specifically instructed otherwise by the Observation Mission's leadership.*]

FOUR

Daniel finds himself in the International Election Observers' office. It's a busy mess with people moving vast quantities of paper around at speed. He stands in the middle of it all with a rucksack on his back and the same pledge in his hand that he read from moments earlier. Fiona enters with a pile of papers.

Fiona You haven't signed it? (*She points.*) The pledge. The code of conduct. You have to sign and print your name, if you want to work as an observer. Do you need a pen?

Daniel Enwehem ike isign iha. [*I can't sign it.*]

Fiona hesitates a moment before launching in.

Fiona Enwebeghim business card. Mana obi eche na gi maka onye m bu. [*I do not have a business card yet. But don't be worried who I am.*]

Daniel Obi adighi echem. amataram ihu gi na press conference. [*I'm not worried. I recognise you from the press conference.*]

Fiona seems confused. Daniel mimes a television screen.

Na TV. [*The TV.*]

Fiona The press conference, you mean? Okay – yes. We always publicly announce our presence in a . . .

Fiona thinks for a moment before pulling out a phrasebook. She reads.

Ihurum mu na TV? [*You saw me on the TV?*]

Daniel Na akuku TV. Ina bata na puta. [*At the side of the screen. You kept bobbing into shot.*]

Fiona Sorry?

Daniel Na bata na puta. [*Bobbing.*]

Fiona I'm sorry I don't –

Lost, Fiona addresses the phrasebook again, but Daniel reaches out and touches the book gently, getting Fiona to raise her eyes and look at him instead. He speaks more slowly now, helping her.

Daniel Bata na puta . . . bata na puta. [*Bobbing . . . bobbing.*]

He begins bobbing up and down. Fiona shakes her head but tries to understand.

Fiona Bata na puta? (*Suddenly it hits her.*) Bobbing?

Fiona copies Daniel and suddenly they are both bobbing up and down.

Bata na puta?

Daniel Bata na puta! Bata na puta!

Fiona Bobbing, yes I see – right.

They both seem extremely pleased with this breakthrough.

I was actually trying to bob out of shot. Trying to. I don't like to see myself on the television.
 Owudighi uchem idi famous na TV. [*It was not my intention to be famous on the TV.*]
 Everyone working as an observer must sign this . . .

Daniel Obu na ekwesirim ibia briefings nile? Ahu adighu nnam, nani mu na ya no, ufodu mgbe mu na atughari ya nga ona eji'e. Amahum ma enwerem ike inye nkwado nile achoro, echerem si odi mpka ka imara. [*Am I expected to attend all the briefings? My father's ill and there's only me and him and so sometimes I have to turn him in his bed. I know that means that I may not be able to provide the kind of support you need but all the same I think it's important for you to know.*]

Fiona says nothing for a moment unsure where to even begin. After a moment she looks down at her phrasebook, lost.

Would you rather we spoke in your language?

Fiona looks at him astonished.

Fiona You speak my language?

Daniel Better than you speak mine.

Fiona You're the translator!

Daniel Yes.

Fiona laughs with relief.

Fiona The Embassy sent me your details. Yes, okay, sorry. And you type?

Daniel Everything. All that you need in terms of paperwork and secretarial support. Will I be with you?

Fiona Sometimes – we have a pool of translators, we grab whoever's available. Why didn't you stop me earlier?

Daniel I wanted to see how hard you'd try. (*He offers his hand.*) Daniel.

Fiona (*she shakes his hand*) Fiona Russell. How was I?

Daniel Not bad. Just about forty-five more regional dialects to go and you won't need me at all.

Fiona smiles and then offers him a pen. Daniel's smile fades, he cannot take the pen.

I can't sign this.

Fiona You know it's not a contract as such. It's a pledge.

Daniel It's still important and I can't sign it.

Fiona May I ask why?

Daniel The section on impartiality . . . that's the problem.

Fiona You are not impartial?

Daniel No. I'm not.

A suited guard arrives at the back of the room. He's chewing on an apple. He checks his watch and takes up his post, standing still except for occasional bites of the apple. Daniel seems unsettled by him. Fiona notices this.

I wouldn't be able to attend all the briefings. My father's very ill and sometimes I have to turn him in his bed.

Fiona We could make an exception.

Daniel looks at the guard as he swallows a mouthful of apple.

Daniel Can he understand us?

Fiona I don't know. I don't think so.

Daniel Does he always just stand there like that?

Fiona Except for lunchtimes. (*She looks at the guard.*) He gets an hour, which is more than enough time to eat lunch but he's always still chewing when he comes back, which makes me wonder what else he does with his hour.

Daniel You think he is having an affair?

Fiona (*she smiles, embarrassed*) What? No. Well, maybe.

Daniel Who is he?

Fiona He's been sent over from one of the party leaderships. They're allowed to watch us. They have access to everything if they want it. To ensure fair play. He's been sent to observe us.

Daniel Observe you?

Fiona Yes, I can understand that it's amusing.

Daniel You've done this job before?

Fiona Many times. We're called in to help with all aspects of elections. Sometimes beforehand, to take the temperature of a country.

Daniel To judge if they're ready?

Fiona Yes. Sometimes to assist with voter registration if a country needs it or will allow us. And, finally, to observe the elections themselves.

Daniel I've been reading everything to be ready. My newspapers, your newspapers – the ones I can get hold of. I wanted to know everything. This election, our first election . . . This is important to me.

Fiona That's good, it should be . . .

Daniel But now I think I know too much. I think we're not ready for this election.

Fiona You are ready.
    Look, if you want to play a part in things then you have to sign the pledge. Then we can get to work . . .

Daniel thinks for a moment and then speaks loudly, testing the guard without looking at him.

Daniel You eat like an animal. You heavy breathe when you eat. Do you hear me?

Fiona watches Daniel, intrigued. The guard does not flinch and clearly cannot understand them. Daniel looks up at Fiona.

Our President, the man who is going to win . . . we deserve better. I really believe that.

Fiona I can't comment on that. And if you sign this pledge neither can you. But you must have come here for a reason.

Daniel My father needs medication. When we are democratic, health organisations will come, won't they?

Fiona Yes.

Daniel With drugs?

Fiona Yes.

Daniel That is why I am here.

Fiona holds out the pen again, Daniel hesitates.

Fiona There's nothing like the excitement of an election night. A first election. I guarantee you'll want to be part of that.

He takes the pen and signs the form, before handing both back to Fiona.

Daniel Do you think there's any chance he might lose?

Fiona No.

FIVE

Saunders walks forward holding a sheaf of emails.

Saunders Intercepted personal email traffic from
Fiona Russell, Deputy Chief of the Observation
Mission, to her husband, Michael Russell.
    'Dear M, I miss you. How are you? I'm knackered
but at least we have almost a full staff now, a week late
but we're getting there.' Personal passages two and four.
Passage three is to be noted and I quote, 'Fabian has
gone and Henrik is in charge now. Well and truly and
doing fine, though there are aspects of the job he hates,
so I've assumed some of the day-to-day management of
the team. You know me, I can't sleep for the minutiae
of it all and that would only be ten times worse if it
was all on my shoulders, or maybe it would be ten
times better. I love your long emails and though I don't
always reply, I do always read them and love them
and laugh hard alone in my little hotel room where
everything is screwed down including the bedside table.'
    Personal passage seven. End of email. Suggest no
action at present time, except continued routine
observation.

SIX

ELECTION DAY, NINE P.M.
HEAVY RAIN EXPECTED IN THE NORTH
AND MOUNTAINOUS REGIONS

*Fiona and Daniel stand in a leaking classroom that's
being used for a polling station. It's raining loudly on*

*a tin roof yet we can hear the growing restlessness of
a large crowd outside. Inside, various containers are
catching large drips of water.*

*Aarya, an observer, enters, pulling down the hood
of a soaking wet cagoule. He moves urgently with a
clipboard in his hand.*

Aarya Abum Aarya, abum onye observer ebe. Otu
onye na-ime ha. [*I'm Aarya, I'm an observer here.
Part of the team.*]

Daniel This is Aarya, he's an observer. Part of the team
at this polling station.

Fiona Pleased to meet you, Aarya, I'm Fiona. I'm
with the International Election Observation –

Aarya Echetaram ya mgbe azuga anyi. [*I remember
her from training.*]

Daniel He remembers you from his induction.

Fiona and Aarya shake hands.

Aarya Osi 9 p.m. akuola, na ikwesighi ino ebe, n'oga
ahu gi. Osi n'oji oru na aka. [*It's after nine p.m. so she
says you have no business being here and that she
won't see you now. She says that she's busy.*]

Daniel He knows why you're here but the head of
the polling station won't see you because it's after
nine p.m.

Fiona It's just a routine visit –

Aarya Ono na ezi na agwa ndi nmadu na polling
station nka na emechi. [*She's outside telling a crowd
of people that this station is closing.*]

Daniel It doesn't matter. She's closing this polling station as we speak. He says there's still a queue of voters out there.

Fiona Tell him we saw the queue –

Daniel Anyi huru nde che ga na ezi. [*We saw the queue out there.*]

Fiona – and that I'll be making a note of it. It's after nine p.m. We should go.

Fiona checks her watch and makes a decision. She picks up her coat.

Aarya Nau anamana? [*You're leaving?*]

Daniel He's asking if we're leaving.

Fiona It's a routine visit but if she won't see us, there's nothing we can do. She's employed by the Central Electoral Committee here. It's her polling station. I'll make a record of it and append it to your report. Thank you, Aarya.

Daniel Oga itinye ya na observation report. Ona ekele gi. [*It'll all be added to your observation report. She's thanking you.*]

Aarya Amaranam, ogwula? [*I can tell, that's it?*]

Daniel Ei, ogwula. [*That's all.*]

Aarya reluctantly hands over his observation report to Fiona, who adds it to a file that she slides back into her bag.

Fiona (*to Aarya*) You're soaked, try and get dry.

Daniel Idere mmiri. [*You're wet.*]

Aarya Odi mma. [*I'm fine.*]

(*Looking around.*) Mmiri zo ga n'ime nga kwa. Agaram akwukwo na ime ulo, Ayi mutara ebe anyi ga eguzo mmiri agaghi ima anyi. [*Now it's raining in here too. I went to school in this room. We learned exactly where to stand, so we wouldn't get dripped on.*]

Daniel He says, now it's raining in here too. He went to school in this room. He remembers exactly where to stand to avoid getting dripped on.

Fiona smiles and takes an umbrella from her bag. She holds out her hand again to be shaken but Aarya won't take it.

Aarya (*suddenly serious*) Please don't go!

Fiona What is it?

Aarya Achorom igwa ya ihe. Odi mma? [*I need to tell her something. Am I allowed?*]

Daniel He wants to tell you something. Kwube. [*Go on.*]

Aarya Mmiri na ezo ma hu na abia na abia. Amaranam 9 p.m. akugo, ma emechie polling station ugbu, nsogbu ga ada. Amam ndia. [*It's just that they keep coming and coming. Despite the weather, and I know it's after nine p.m., but I really think that if they close the polling station now there will be trouble. I know these people.*]

Daniel He says despite the weather people keep coming and coming. He thinks there'll be trouble if they turn people away. If they close this station. He says he knows these people.

Fiona I can't keep the polling station open. It's not up to me. I have no power here.

Daniel Onwehi ike ebee. [*She has no power here.*]

Aarya Onye ma. [*I doubt that.*]

Daniel He doubts that.

Fiona What is it . . . what's he seen today? Has there been trouble?

Daniel Kwube. [*Go on.*]

Aarya speaks and Daniel simultaneously translates.

Aarya Akwara otu nwoke aka iwe. Umu nwoke abuo luru ogu na 6.53 p.m. Otu nwanyi kpega ekpere mere ujo abiatu nmadu, si 7.30 ruo 7.50 p.m. Okpechaa, ya evoto, lawa. [*One man was pushed. Two other men fought one another at 6.53 p.m. A woman praying made people uneasy. That was from 7.30 to 7.50 p.m. After that she voted and left.*]

Daniel 'One man was shoved. Two men fought each other at 6.53 p.m. A woman wouldn't stop praying which made people uneasy. That was from 7.30 p.m. to 7.50 p.m., then she voted and left.'

Fiona (*to Aarya*) To be honest that sounds perfectly normal. Look, the reports will be gathered up and I'll read everything you've written, my team and I will. Thank you for your work here today Aarya. Dalu. [*Thank you.*] Daniel would you –

Aarya (*urgently*) Imerime ndi bia ivotu ga eji ukwu abia; n'ime obodo ka esi hu, otutu ije ruru six miles, ke hu ga ebido mgbe hu a gbasara oru. [*Most of these* *voters have walked from the countryside. It's six miles but they would have walked after work, started off after work.*]

Daniel These are rural voters, and most of them have come from six miles away. They've walked here.

Fiona There was a problem with the boundary lines drawn up by your Electoral Committee. They cut villages in half. Some people had to walk a few feet to vote, these people a few miles.

Aarya Obi adighi ha mma na ekere ha uzo abuo, ufodu ga alaghachi nabalia, lite na isi ututu, ga oru. [*They were unhappy about being split in two. Some people have to walk back tonight and then they'll get up and work tomorrow.*]

Daniel People have work tomorrow and yet they will walk back tonight. Six miles here and six miles home.

Aarya Onweghi ihe owe ike ime? [*Is there nothing she can do?*]

Daniel He asks is there nothing you can do?

Fiona thinks for a moment. She glances at her watch. She's torn.

Fiona They should have put a person in the queue at nine p.m. A marker. Does he know who that person is?

Daniel Mgbe 9 p.m. kuru, ha gara itinye nmadu na ime line. [*At nine p.m. they should have placed someone in the queue.*]

Aarya Mba ha etinye hu. [*They didn't.*]

Daniel No, that didn't happen.

Fiona No one was placed in the queue at nine p.m.? No one from inside this polling station?

Daniel No.

Fiona Ask him how many people arrived after nine p.m.

Daniel Nmadu ole banyere na line mgbe 9 p.m. kuchara? [*How many people outside joined the queue would you say, after nine p.m.?*]

Aarya Enweghim ike ikwucha. Mga asi, enwerike ke oha uzo abuo. [*It's impossible to say. At least half.*]

Daniel At least half of the queue arrived after nine p.m.

Fiona And now it's 9.41 . . .

Daniel Are you asking me?

Fiona Sorry no, I'm thinking aloud. We really have to go, but . . .

Daniel You're thinking that the polling station shouldn't be closed?

Aarya Ha na abia na abia, ha bia gidere si ehihie. [*They just keep coming and coming. They've been coming like this for hours.*]

Daniel He says it's been a steady stream of people for hours now.

Fiona Okay . . . (*She thinks and looks at her watch.*) Okay. I need to speak to whoever's in charge of this polling station first.

Daniel She won't see you.

Fiona Tell her I'm not going until she does. Can you ask Aarya to find her, please?

Daniel Ga gwa onye isi, si ya na anyi agaghi ala, tupu anyi ahu ya. [*Get whoever is in charge here. Tell her we're not going till she comes.*]

Aarya nods and disappears outside into the rain. Daniel watches Fiona. She gazes up at the leaking roof which is now dripping on her and puts up her umbrella.

Daniel That's bad luck.

Fiona It'll be worse luck if I catch a cold. You're the one stuck in a jeep with me.

Daniel He's right, you know. There could be trouble here tonight. These people want to cast a vote. Desperately.

Fiona Are you really so surprised by that?

Daniel I just never imagined so many. You have reports like this from other polling stations?

Fiona Yes, but I'm not too worried. Not until I get all the observation reports back, then we'll really have a fuller picture of the whole region.

Daniel Then you'll know if it was valid? A proper election?

Fiona (*calmly looking at him*) It's your election. We just issue a statement, a preliminary post-election statement of our findings.

Daniel Your observations?

Fiona Yes, but it's your election.

Daniel But you will decide if the world judges it a fair contest or not. We're only valid if you say so.

Fiona People take an interest in what we have to say . . . I think that's fair enough.

Aarya re-enters, followed by Kalifa, head of this polling station.

Kalifa Oforo nwobere ya kuo 10 p.m. Otu hour aga'la mgbe ayi kwesiri imechi. *Abia hu hu n'oge.* [*It is nearly ten o'clock. It is an hour after it should have closed. They are too late.*]

Fiona shows her identification badge and then pulls out her passport which she holds up to Kalifa, keeping it visible at all times.

Fiona I'm the Deputy Chief of the International –

Kalifa I understand, but it is too late now, don't you think? We waited an hour because we felt that was fair.

Fiona You're supposed to put a marker in the queue and then you tell people that no one beyond that person is allowed to vote. That's the common practice.

Kalifa It was our job to arrange that?

Fiona Yes it was. It's your polling station.

Kalifa Those people cannot vote now.

Daniel They've walked six miles.

Kalifa I know how far they've come. What am I supposed to do? I gave people an extra hour. I can't move people through any quicker.

Fiona The fact that the admin is slow is not their fault.

Kalifa Gini? [*What?*]

Fiona pulls Kalifa to one side, under her umbrella. Daniel watches.

Fiona The fact that the paperwork takes time is hardly their fault.

Kalifa (*more firmly*) But turning up after nine p.m. is. After we are closed.

Fiona How do you know who turned up after nine p.m. without a marker in the queue? These people could have been here for hours. They have a right to vote.

Kalifa What do you recommend?

Fiona You remain open. You don't close. You don't want a scene at a polling station. Your station. Other places will have the same problem tonight. The boundary lines have been marked badly. Huge amounts of people will be travelling tonight. You won't be the only station open all night.

Kalifa looks at Fiona for a moment. An uneasy transaction passes between them, which Kalifa wrestles with.

Kalifa And your observation? What will you write?

Fiona As long as these people have a chance to vote then nothing that we write will be a problem I'm sure.

Kalifa turns and walks back outside the polling station. After a moment, we hear a small cheer

*from the crowd outside before the hint of laughing
and excitement.*

*Aarya nods at Fiona and smiles, heading out to
see for himself.*

Aarya Dalu! Dalu! [*Thank you! Thank you!*]

*Daniel steps back over to Fiona who has pulled out
a mobile phone. She pulls a second one from
another pocket and transfers a number from one
to the other.*

Fiona We'll make a move now. Head along this route
and keep going. We have to make up some time.

Daniel These people are from the countryside.

Fiona I know.

Daniel You know they favour one side.

Fiona You can't say that for sure.

Daniel Most of them at this time of night, from the
country, will favour one party very clearly. By leaving
the polling station open could you not be said to be
favouring one side?

Fiona These people deserve to vote. No one wants
violence. And this is just one polling station.

Daniel But still, you could make that argument.

Fiona Yes you could.

Blackout. The rain slowly stops.

SEVEN

Saunders steps forward with a manila folder in his hand.

Saunders 'I leave the hotel and I get into a car and I get out of a car and walk straight into our office. I've been here three weeks and it feels like I've barely set foot in this country . . . until today. You didn't call me, Michael. Did you forget? People actually queued, sat on boxes, held their children, waited patiently and then cast their vote. Their first ever vote. I know I'm supposed to be all cool and considered about it by now, and I have some idea how boring this must be for you after twelve years, but I am constantly amazed by people's hunger to mark a cross in a box. Whenever I feel shitty and miles away I have to bear that in mind. I hope you do too.'

Passage three carries details of some interest, the description of a minor civil disturbance and her perceived bias of the state-owned TV station favouring the incumbent President. It also appears she met the Ambassador at a formal dinner to which I wasn't invited. That's fine, I just mention it, that's all. Passage four concludes: 'The next forty-eight hours will be a blur so I may not be in touch again for a little while.' Love etc., end of email.

Regarding shopping. There are certain things that I struggle to get so please send hand cream and cotton buds as my hands are dry and my ears are dirty. Go ahead and have a big laugh in the office on me, just as long as you send them. Sincerely, Saunders.

EIGHT

ELECTION NIGHT, THREE A.M.
THE FINAL COUNTS POUR IN

Fiona enters followed by Tony, an American and a member of the Observation Team, and Edi, French and also a member of the team. While Tony and Fiona speak, Edi sets up her laptop and waits somewhat impatiently.

Tony I'm thinking, if we're not ready, my vote is for holding off, you know. Not rushing out a preliminary report just to meet a deadline.

Fiona We have to be ready. The press conference is nine a.m. tomorrow

Tony (*getting edgy*) Sure, but if the report isn't finished, Fiona –

Fiona It will be.

Tony We're still writing it. We're still waiting for key results, for –

Fiona In every observation mission I've ever been on, in every election, this always happens.

Tony Sure, and I know we've never worked together before . . . But with all due respect, this is my fifth mission in twelve months, Fiona –

Fiona And this is my twenty-eighth observation mission in almost twelve years, Tony. I know what I'm doing. We keep writing, we keep working. We'll be ready. We have to be. People want to know what we think.

Tony And what do we think?

Fiona We'll work it out . . . together.

Tony looks at Fiona and Edi.

Tony Look, I'm sorry okay . . . I'm just tired and a bit pissed off, that's all. It looks like he's gonna win . . . and in the first round too. I mean, why?

Edi People must have voted for him.

Tony (*wryly*) Of course. I forgot that's how it worked.

Fiona gathers her notes and Edi spots that she looks ready to start.

Edi Where's Henrik?

Tony Schmoozing. He's on a top table at some dinner thing.

Fiona It's an official function!

Tony It's three a.m.

Fiona I'm sure he's on his way.

Edi Well . . . should we start?

Fiona considers this for half a moment.

Fiona Tony . . .?

Tony (*reading*) 'International Election Observation Mission. Presidential Election.'

Fiona I trust you on the title page, Tony.

Tony Okay . . .

Edi's fingers hover over the laptop. Tony prepares himself before he speaks.

In the course of this next exchange all three of them speak sparingly from notes but largely in the moment as they begin to shape a document, which Edi types up and which we'll see appear on a screen behind her. There is a sense they are performing for one another, so point-scoring and general one-upmanship is rife.

Tony suddenly begins in a burst of fluency. Edi's fingers dance up and down, capturing every word.

Tony 'This statement of preliminary findings and conclusions is delivered prior to the completion of the electoral process. An overall assessment of the entire election will be dependent in part on the conduct of the remaining phases of the process. The International Mission will publish a final report presenting a comprehensive analysis of all observer findings approximately one month after the completion of that process.' (*He looks up.*) Then we've got the 'Institutions Represented' page.

Fiona Okay. Let's go on then. Preliminary Conclusions. Edi?

Edi 'Despite improvements in the administration of the election carried out in the pre-election period, the Presidential contest still did not achieve the highest standards set for democratic elections. The Central Electoral Committee, or CEC, administered the election in a generally transparent manner.'

Tony Are we happy with 'generally'? Because we went back and forth on it.

Edi 'In the main'? 'By and large'?

Fiona 'Generally' is fine.

Tony Happy with 'generally'.

Edi (*going on*) 'State media largely met their legal obligations –'

Tony Happy with 'largely'?

Fiona nods.

Edi '. . . largely met their obligations to provide free airtime to candidates. However, overall media bias in favour of the incumbent diminished the possibility for electors to make fully informed choices.'

Fiona Tony – what went well?

Tony One, 'On 9th November, the President in his capacity as Head of State but at the same time a prospective candidate, issued a decree which stated the intention to conduct a free, fair and competitive election.'

Edi Two. 'Most lower-level election staff appeared well-trained and equipped.'

Tony Three. 'A debate among the five presidential candidates was broadcast live on television with state-wide coverage.'

Edi 'Although the incumbent chose not to participate, thus reducing the value of this event for the electorate.'

Daniel bursts in, apologetically.

Daniel Another two districts are in. Both in favour of the President.

Fiona Not even close?

Daniel No, not really.

Tony How many results are in?

Daniel Forty to forty-five. Do you want me to keep sticking my head in?

Fiona Could you?

Daniel No problem.

Fiona How are you holding up?

Daniel An hour ago I was ready to collapse but you were right . . . just being here as it happens. It's amazing. Thank you.

Daniel disappears and Fiona watches him go, proudly.

Edi (*pushing on*) 'The election process revealed a number of shortcomings. There was evidence of pressure exerted on students by university faculties to vote in favour of the incumbent.'

Fiona Stop. Don't type that. We spoke about this.

Edi I know.

Fiona I thought we spoke about this, Edi. I thought we agreed to leave it out.

Edi (*strong*) We had more reports from –

Tony I read all the reports, all the observations made, it didn't change my opinion. It's a weak argument.

Edi Kids were being coerced. There was harassment, intimidation.

Tony *Some* intimidation. Look I know it's not healthy but it's the way things are done out here right now.

Edi Not by the opposition. He's progressive, moderate.

Tony Two very good reasons why he's in opposition.

Edi Look, 'They were being pressured by their rectors and professors to vote in the election, and occasionally to vote for the incumbent President.'

Tony 'Occasionally'? A word like that is no use at all. It's vague, it's speculative.

Edi So pick another word, but this belongs in there. These kids –

Tony They're adults, they're not kids. They can vote. They're students, not kids.

Edi Students were detained, then. Okay. Some of them were forced to eat the opposition party placards they'd been holding. To eat them, for God's sake. (*Appealing.*) Fiona?

Fiona I know . . .

Edi And campaign staff and supporters of opposition candidates, call them what you want, but some of them were beaten.

Tony Two were beaten.

Edi For fuck sake, that's still two. And how many more were coerced? I don't believe this.

Fiona (*a steady hand*) Okay, adults were being coerced. Students were. I don't doubt it. But what did it affect?

Tony Even if ten students were coerced –

Edi Try thirty-two.

Tony If thirty-two were coerced, then. Does it have an effect on the outcome? Palpably, I mean. Don't we have to choose our targets more carefully? If we report things that don't affect the outcome of this election then we're not helping anyone to get a clear picture.

Edi It makes a pretty clear picture to me!

Fiona (*genuine, to Edi*) It's terrible, two students being beaten is terrible . . . but it doesn't mean this wasn't a democratic election. In the grand scheme of things – these details really aren't important.

Edi Do you honestly believe that?

Fiona Yes, I do. I have to. (*She falters.*) We have to always keep the bigger picture in mind. I know that might seem harsh.

Tony Edi, nobody wants to buy this guy a beer, but that doesn't mean he belongs in The Hague either. Let's be clear. We are saying this election was free and fair. Because despite all this . . . I'm convinced. Fiona?

Edi and Tony look at Fiona. She hesitates for a moment.

Fiona Yes, of course. What's next?

Tony Okay, so 'Voting was conducted in a generally calm atmosphere.'

Edi Discounting the beatings and a general everyday sense of coercion.

Fiona (*lightly*) Edi!

Edi It's out of my system now, I promise.

Fiona 'Legal Framework'?

Edi It's pro-forma mostly. There's 'The Law on Peaceful Assemblies' section, which is new.

Daniel bursts back in, completely forgetting he is holding a tupperware box with a fork sticking out of it.

Daniel Two more districts are in.

Fiona Town or rural?

Daniel Town, and the President got the highest share of the vote but nowhere near as strong as the exit polls suggested. The gap to the main opposition has definitely closed a little.

Tony (*nodding at what Daniel is holding*) What's that?

Daniel (*realising*) Pinto beans with potatoes . . .

They look at him enviously before Daniel pulls back and exits.

Tony 'Co-operation of the Military and the Police'?

Edi (*dry*) What co-operation?

Fiona I was supposed to meet with them, some liaison officer. They never returned my calls.

Tony Well, should we mention that?

Fiona There's no point. It's not helpful. Move on.

Edi Tony and I made a bet about this next thing. If you keep it in, he buys me dinner.

Tony If you throw it out, we trade rooms. Hers is bigger than mine and the lamp isn't screwed down. I'm sick to death of reading on the john.

Fiona What is it?

Edi 'As required by the Law on Peaceful Assemblies, candidates had to seek permission for open meetings with voters ten days in advance of the event. Of the fifty-one requests made countrywide, only five meetings were approved and only one in the requested location.'
What do you think?

They both watch Fiona who takes a moment.

Fiona Who grants the requests for these meetings? I mean, who stood in the way?

Edi The Central Electoral Committee.

Fiona Okay. (*She thinks.*) Leave it in.

Edi (*amazed*) Really?

Tony Fuck!

Fiona People were prevented from meeting in public, Tony. That's notable, really notable. (*To Edi.*) Leave it exactly as you wrote it.

Declan enters with a flourish. He is immaculately well presented in a brushed-cotton jacket and chinos with tissue paper in his collar to guard against his fresh make-up smudging his shirt. He immediately looks alien in the room.

Declan He's done it! He's clung on!

Fiona Declan.

Declan Fiona. I was closer than I thought. Jumped in a Subaru and here we are. He's done it.

Fiona We're still getting the results in. My understanding is that it's narrowing a bit, but –

Declan I've seen the exits. He's done enough, I think.

Fiona We should hold on.

Declan (*ignoring this, as he works his way round the room*) You know, you wait up all bloody night and all they do is moan back at the office. They want footage, they want a report. They want to know something.

Fiona Everybody does.

Declan (*looking straight at Fiona*) Can I have a word?

Fiona flashes a look at Tony and Edi and they leave slowly. After a moment Declan and Fiona are alone. There's a strange tension between them. The laptop remains open. Declan spots this and slowly edges towards it during their conversation.

Fiona Declan?

Declan Fiona – don't make that face. You look like a disappointed parent.

Fiona I am.

Declan (*playful*) Disappointed? In me? Look, if the exits are saying something loud and clear then you have to listen. I do, anyway.

Fiona It's not exactly loud and clear though, is it?

Declan My information is. You've been holed up here since the polls closed. You should take in the night. There's a feeling on the streets.

Fiona Will you wait?

Declan Honestly? No. I'm doing a live report in eight minutes. And they want to hear something. Which I have. But I need another figure to back it up.

Fiona From me?

Declan From you. I have one. This guy I know has seen an exit poll that puts the President unassailably ahead. Returns him to office in the first round.

Fiona Ours don't, and there are thousands more votes to tally.

Declan My guy says it won't make a difference. It's not expected to affect the outcome.

Fiona He knows the way that thousands of people have voted?

Declan I know. Fucking arrogant, isn't it? So if you let me have the figure you've got – then I can feed it into what I say.

Fiona (*wising up to him*) I see.

Declan For balance.

Declan looks at the laptop. Fiona steps over and closes it. They stand over it, facing one another now.

Fiona We'll be making a preliminary statement in the morning.

Declan It is the morning.

Fiona We have to be careful. First-time elections are extremely delicate. Also, some key standards weren't met.

Declan (*excited*) You're not going to say the election was void . . .? Because I mean *that* is a story.

Fiona No that's not what we're going to say. It was free and fair . . . enough.

Declan Well then?

Fiona You can't call this election, not yet.

Declan I am not calling this election. The people are. You said it yourself. Free and fair . . . enough. Let the will of the people prevail. Give me your figure and I'll have both sides of the story.

Fiona (*playful*) You need that for a responsible report, do you?

Declan (*straight*) I'm a good journalist.

Fiona Declan . . .

Declan Fiona . . .

Fiona Wait an hour. (*Trying to accommodate him.*) Look, it's close. What if I said that on air?

Declan An interview with you? Sweetheart, that's thrilling, but who are you? You're not exactly newsworthy. Where's Henrik? I could use Henrik.

Fiona Henrik is at dinner.

Declan It's three in the morning. So once again the tireless deputy does all the work but gets none of the credit. I heard you got passed over again. You should propose a coup.

Fiona *Propose* a coup? I'm not sure that's how they work. What will your report say?

Declan (*with his news voice*) 'And while a democratic mandate for this President seemed unpalatable to many in the West, here on the ground the worsening economic climate has led people to opt for a safe pair of hands.' (*Back to his normal voice.*) And we've actually got a pair of hands to cut to at that point, you know, holding a voting slip.

Fiona (*dry*) Brilliant.

Declan Magical, isn't it?

Fiona Seriously, that's it?

Declan What more do you want? We're not all John fucking Simpson. Mere mortals get a minute and a half of tape and two questions with the smug bastard in the studio that nicked my job. You're not the only one who's been cruelly passed over, you know. I too am stuck on this seemingly never-ending democracy-sort-of concert tour.

Fiona Declan. One hour. Please.

Declan You know, tonight's the night. The eyes of the world are watching. By the morning they'll be looking somewhere else. You know how this works. Give me something. (*Becoming annoyed.*) May I remind you, you're supposed to be transparent?

Fiona We are transparent.

Declan Just because your boy didn't win.

Fiona What did you say?

Declan It's understandable. I feel the same. He's much more appetising than the President. Moderate, dare

39

I say – sincere. But he's losing, and that's the script for tonight, Fiona. Roll with it.

Fiona laughs at him. She laughs long and hard.

Fiona Roll with it? My boy, is he? How dare you! I've slept six hours in the past two days ensuring anyone, anyone can vote. I don't care who for.

Declan Yes you do. Of course you do. So do I.

Fiona Don't treat me like an idiot, Declan. I don't want a picture created that might then change – it gives the incumbent an advantage. It's not the done thing. You know that.

Daniel bursts back in.

Daniel Sixty-two per cent of the vote is in. But it's really tight and it's getting tighter because it's the villages – the rural districts, I mean – that are trickling in last and they're all leaning towards the opposition leader. It's closing things up between the two of them. The President's still in front, but he can't win it in the first round. Not if it carries on like this.

Daniel realises Fiona is with a member of the press. He worries he has said something out of turn. Fiona looks at Declan who is smiling widely back at her.

Fiona I'm going to ask you to pretend that you didn't hear that.

Declan I'll be honest with you, Fee, perfectly truthful, right? Covering this election has been a real low point in my career. Like someone was trying to tell me something, you know – professionally. So imagine the surprise of suddenly finding myself in the middle of something mildly interesting or at the absolute, very least, broadcastable.

Fiona Just wait an hour . . . please.

NINE

ELECTION NIGHT, FOUR A.M.
A DEAD HEAT PROJECTED

A public square. Declan steps forward and strips the tissue from his collar. As he goes 'on air' his voice alters, while his face is projected onto the screen behind.

Declan Behind me you may be able to hear the bleating of car horns and more than the odd firework. The picture here is fractured and certainly incomplete as I speak to you, but as the results continue to drip in slowly all reports point to the likelihood of a real upset here tonight. Voter turnout was encouraging. It could have been much higher, but certainly no one expected this contest to limp beyond a first round. That now seems increasingly likely with the incumbent President ahead of his main rival in the polls but not by enough to clinch a first-round win.

It's expected that just two candidates will now go forward to a second round run-off. The one thing we can say with confidence is that this divided country, divided when it went to the polls, remains divided still tonight. I have with me Henrik Mickelson, Chief of the International Election Observation Mission, who kindly joins me from an official dinner marking this historic occasion. Henrik?

TEN

ELECTION NIGHT, LATER:
INTERNATIONAL OBSERVERS' PRELIMINARY
STATEMENT DUE SHORTLY

A man in a dinner suit runs in and rugby-tackles Fiona to the ground and the papers she's holding go flying. The two of them wrestle on the floor. It soon becomes apparent that the man is trying to get Fiona's watch off her.

After a struggle and much rolling around on the paper-strewn floor, he manages to remove it from Fiona's wrist. The man stands, triumphant and breathless, before laying the watch on the floor and stamping on it. He smiles sweatily at Fiona.

Henrik (*still breathless*) Swedish Arctic reindeer meat. Drambuie. Hot-buttered toast. A glass of Cognac.

Fiona Toast?

Henrik I know, but in the context of the reindeer meat it was perfect. I didn't drink. Not the Drambuie. I had the Cognac.

Fiona (*reaching into her pocket*) Henrik, you still have to take this phone call, you know.

Henrik That's why I didn't drink. (*He looks at her.*) We're in for the long haul, then. Seconds away, round two, and I haven't brought nearly enough underpants. I'm going to whack some on expenses – feel free to do the same. Did you ever imagine it would go to a second round?

Fiona No. Not for a moment.

Henrik Me neither. I thought I'd get a nice easy gig, this first time. A little landslide maybe. Now what we write actually matters.

Fiona It always matters . . . (*Warmly.*) You'll be fine.

Fiona holds out a mobile phone and Henrik takes it carefully, before straightening himself up and trying to make an effort. He is tense, full of nervous energy.

Henrik So tell me, then? How are we looking?

Fiona We're in good shape.

Henrik How's the team? Our little international family? We're Mummy and Daddy, you do realise that?

Fiona (*smiling*) They're okay. Knackered but –

Henrik And the report?

Fiona I'm happy with it. We faxed it to Geneva, for sign-off.

Henrik That's good.

Fiona They'll call. It'll be any second.

Henrik And I just need to . . .?

Fiona You just need to walk them through the preliminary report. Check that they're happy with it before you do the press conference.

Henrik When is the press conference?

Fiona Four hours or so. (*She looks at her wrist but her watch is gone.*)

Henrik Gotcha.

Fiona But first you need to take the call.

Henrik They're bound to have notes.

Fiona They always do.

Henrik Stick around, will you? Just in case . . .

Henrik takes a deep breath and looks at the mobile anxiously. Fiona watches him.

I feel like a pin-up. A sort of greying Norwegian political pin-up. But what can I do – I have a soft face. That's why they wanted me.

Fiona You smile a lot certainly. People like that about you.

Henrik I'm safe and I have a soft face. You've got a hard face.

Fiona I've been doing this a long time.

Henrik Which is why you should be doing *my* job. I want you to know that I know that, Fiona.

Fiona Thank you.

She sits on the floor. Henrik relaxes.

Henrik I was thinking, at dinner . . . between the reindeer and the dessert . . . we never talk about home.

Fiona You and I?

Henrik Any of us. Our lives back home. Why is that, do you think?

Fiona What's to talk about?

Henrik Exactly! It doesn't exist for people like us any more does it? Six years I've been doing all this. One election after another. I have no friends any more. My boyfriend's left me, I think. It's never-ending isn't it? And you've been doing it even longer than I have. You're married, aren't you?

Fiona Yes. Just about. If emails count.

Henrik That bad, is it?

Fiona (*reluctant*) When we see each other it's fine, good. But this job . . . I just think we value things very differently, maybe.

Henrik What does that mean?

Fiona My being here, doing this. Being away from home. I don't know that Michael really gets it or . . . I don't know. Can we not talk about it?

Henrik Of course. Friends?

Fiona One or two.

Henrik And do you talk to them any more? What do you talk about? I mean, where's the common ground? Don't you find this job has ruined you? What are we doing here, Fiona?

Fiona looks at him and bursts out laughing, Henrik laughs too.

Fiona Just the one brandy, was it?

Henrik Talk to me. Please talk to me. I feel like I haven't had a proper conversation for six years, not one without a bloody translator, anyway. Talk about anything at all. We've got until this phone rings.

Fiona I can't . . . seem to allow myself to stop and think. I don't know why that is.

Henrik Because to you thinking is a luxury. And you've got a job to do, so you feel guilty.

Fiona That's right, I do.

Henrik But it's me. So just talk . . . Be as undiplomatic as you like, be indiscreet. What are you thinking right now? Fiona!

Fiona I don't know.
 I wonder why you broke my watch.

Henrik (*happy – he had almost forgotten*) I've bought you a new watch. To say thank you for babysitting me. That's why I wanted to talk to you, to tell you that. But you already had a watch.

Fiona So you broke it?

Henrik You'll like your new one better, trust me. What else?

> *There's a long pause. Fiona looks at Henrik. She seems to want to say something but she doesn't. She can't. She fights with it a little more and then speaks.*

Fiona I'm not really sleeping . . .

Henrik (*transfixed*) Go on.

Fiona I can't stop thinking about . . . voter registration.

Henrik Oh my God, that is the saddest thing I've ever heard!

Fiona We're talking. You said whatever was on my mind.

Henrik Okay. I did. Fair enough. Go on . . .

Fiona Look, the registration was poor, but still the turnout was more than we expected and consequently the result has been tighter than we expected.

Henrik That's the way it goes.

Fiona Their Electoral Committee didn't do its job. The forms were cluttered with text, they asked the same question several different ways, some people didn't know if they were registered or not. They didn't know if they could vote –

Henrik You could be talking about any country on earth.
   Don't stop. What else?

Fiona (*looking at him closely*) Is it possible that . . . (*She hesitates.*)

Henrik What? Say it . . .

Fiona Is it possible that more people could be registered between the first round and the second round of this election?

Henrik That's what you're asking me? Could more people be registered?

Fiona Yes.

   Henrik leans back and considers.

Henrik There's an argument you could make to the Central Electoral Committee here, if you had to. They have an Article 32, it's very simple. Quite clean: 'Every citizen who has reached the age of eighteen shall be entitled to vote and be elected to a public office. The voting right is exercised at the elections.'

Fiona Elections? With an 's'. It says that?

Henrik Yes.

Fiona People have a right to vote.

Henrik Of course.

Fiona Which means people have a right to be registered to vote all the time there is an election for them to vote in.

Henrik You could make that argument.

Fiona (*a quiet urgency*) *We* could.

> *Henrik looks at her. He seems uncomfortable under her gaze.*

I was lecturing them, the team. Trying to convince them, you know: 'This is the job.' 'These things are just a part of the process.'

Henrik What things?

Fiona The brutalities.

Henrik They are.

Fiona I know, I know that . . . I just . . . I'm not sure.

Henrik I think you have to remember why we're here.

Fiona I know why we're here and I keep repeating that to myself. I do. But we were also supposed to come here and see this little country take a huge step forward, albeit with the wrong man in charge. That was what was supposed to happen. But it hasn't. Despite every advantage he's had as President, everything at his disposal, he hasn't won it –

48

Henrik Yet.

Fiona He hasn't won it in the first round. What if this country is ready to take two huge steps forward, and they just need our help . . .

Fiona looks at Henrik closely. There is a strange tension between them.

Henrik How many more voters would it take? Hypothetically?

Fiona The second round is in fifteen days.

Henrik How many?

Fiona Fifty thousand.

Henrik And that would make a difference?

Fiona In a country this size, maybe. I don't know. If you got us a bit more money from Geneva, then –

Henrik laughs, but Fiona pushes on.

It would have to be in concord with the Electoral Committee here, of course.

Henrik I can't see them agreeing to that.

Fiona Why not?

Henrik They were appointed by the President.

Fiona Not directly. And they sit on a committee spearheading democratic reform. They must want that.

Henrik (*knowingly*) Fiona. Who are you trying to register?

Fiona People who aren't already registered.

Henrik But where are you going to start? We have fifteen days. In the country? In the city?

Fiona Both.

Henrik Both? We don't have time.

Fiona (*a reluctant admission*) Well, the rural areas are more disenfranchised, you know that.

Henrik This is making a statement, you know.

Fiona So is not registering people. It's the same statement. They cancel each other out.

Henrik Do they?

Fiona (*strong*) I want people to vote.

Henrik And if that means affecting the outcome?

Fiona Yes. If that means change, then . . . I mean, you know, if that's what people want . . .

Fiona looks at Henrik.

Henrik You know this is taking advantage of my lack of experience and generally appalling leadership skills.

Fiona That and the fact you've been drinking.

Henrik (*dry*) Thank you for your honesty.
   If I agreed, who would go to the Electoral Committee here?

Fiona I would.

Henrik I could tell Geneva that?

Fiona Yes.

Henrik You're a lawyer?

Fiona No. I could take a lawyer – for what it's worth. I'll just be reading their constitution back to them. They'll either go for it or they won't. It's not illegal.

The phone in Henrik's hand rings.

Henrik I'm not convinced, Fiona . . .

He stands and answers it. Fiona stands too.

(*Into the phone.*) Thank you, I'll hold on. (*He covers the handset.*) Time's up.

Fiona None of the briefing notes I read before I came made me feel like this at all. Then you arrive on the ground and . . . something changes.

Henrik is listening closely, Fiona hesitates.

No one expected it to be this close. But it is. And now we have a perfectly legal, proper and honest opportunity to effect a change.

Henrik We're just here as observers.

Fiona People walked for six miles to vote. I've been doing this job for twelve years and I'm telling you that for the first time in what feels like a lifetime we can do something real here. Something genuine. That opportunity may not come again. I don't feel bad about taking it and neither should you.

Henrik If only it could come from them. If only it were their idea . . .

Fiona Would that really make any difference?

Henrik thinks about this for a moment before indicating the phone.

Henrik Okay. I'll put it to them. Now I know why we don't talk – you get me into trouble.

ELEVEN

Saunders looks a little smarter now and more alert.

Saunders The President's failure to win in the first round has shocked everyone and there's quite a hum of expectation in the bars and cafés around town. No one quite knows how serious it is, or if he'll simply rally back in the next round and crush the opposition. Things are calm now and will remain so, all the time the President is ahead.

Continued personal email traffic from Fiona Russell to Michael Russell suggests she is now to all intents and purposes in charge, day-to-day, of the International Observation team, and, I quote: 'Henrik seems amenable to it, relieved even. We are keeping up appearances, with him attending briefings while I run the operational side.' A date has been set between Fiona Russell and the Central Electoral Committee here, an emergency meeting concerning the second round. Why? What is she up to? Her tone in these past few emails to her husband is markedly more emotional than before, combative even. I quote: 'I know you've never fully understood why I do this job. But please believe me when I say that this is the most important place I can be right now.'

I've tried to get a moment of the Ambassador's time but what with his diary and me arranging a bloody marquee for the Queen's Birthday Party . . . Look, I know it's unorthodox but I really feel the time has come for someone, for me, to make contact with Fiona Russell . . . though I of course await your instructions.

Also, my most recent parcel was received with some of the contents damaged. The damson jam was fine but the gooseberry had cracked and gone everywhere. Can you get whoever packs the diplomatic bag to please wrap more carefully next time. Sincerely, Saunders.

TWELVE

FOURTEEN DAYS UNTIL THE SECOND-ROUND RUN-OFF: TWO CANDIDATES REMAIN

Daniel lights two candles on a small table. His father, Muturi, steps in behind him, leaning on a chunky walking stick. He watches his son. Daniel steps back from the table and takes in his handywork. In the soft light we see it is laid for dinner.

Muturi Wete radio ahu. [*Get the radio.*]

Daniel slips out as his father steps towards the table and looks proudly at the setting. After a moment Fiona steps in with a clinking plastic bag. Muturi looks up at her and she smiles and is about to speak when he holds up his hand to silence her. Fiona seems surprised as, just then, Daniel enters with the radio and sees Fiona. He too is about to speak but his father stops him also. Muturi holds out his hand for the radio, which Daniel gives him. He switches it on and slides the dial before setting it on the corner of the table. Classical music filters out, tinny and a little broken but beautiful nonetheless.

Now . . . we're ready. I'm Muturi.

Fiona smiles and steps forward. She shakes his hand.

Fiona Thank you. For having me – this is really kind of you.

Daniel Have a seat.

Fiona I have a driver outside.

Muturi He'll be fine. Let him sleep.

Fiona Is that okay?

Muturi We'll give him a doggy bag after.

Fiona places the clinking plastic bag down on the table.

Fiona I meant to get wine, but time has been –

Muturi Daniel tells me. You are running around. You're busy.

Fiona Well, we all are.

Muturi I'm not busy.

Fiona I brought these. Emptied my mini-bar.

She starts unpacking miniatures. Daniel laughs. Muturi seems confused.

Muturi Mini-bar?

Fiona In my hotel. In my room.

Muturi picks up a bottle.

Muturi But they're tiny.

Fiona Expensive too.

Muturi Then you mustn't –

Fiona No, no, I didn't mean . . . It's fine. I wanted to. It's the least I could do.

Daniel Have a seat.

Fiona sits, so does Muturi. Daniel picks up the miniature bottles and looks at them.

Fiona This is lovely.

Daniel You haven't tasted the food yet. It'll be ready soon.

Fiona No rush.

They sit and listen to the music for a moment. Muturi picks up a tiny bottle and reads the label.

Muturi 'Gordon's Gin'!

Fiona takes the bottle from him and unscrews the lid. She pours it into a cup. Muturi watches her.

You were supposed to be gone home by now?

Fiona We didn't think it would go to a second round.

Muturi I saw you on television, in the corner of the screen. I told my neighbour, I said we have a celebrity coming for food, he tried to invite himself over, him and his wife.

Daniel Dad got a bit protective.

Muturi She's our celebrity. (*Looking at the cup.*) What is that?

Fiona has taken out a tiny can of tonic and poured it into the cup. She picks up a knife from the table and stirs it.

Fiona Bar's open. (*To Muturi.*) Gin and tonic, for you.

Daniel He doesn't –

Muturi I won't. I'm afraid. It's bad for my blood.

Daniel His anaemia.

Fiona Of course, I'm sorry.

Muturi Agwala ya ihe anakpo ya! [*Don't tell her what it's called!*]

Daniel She already knows.

Muturi You give something a name and it always sounds worse. As if his cooking wasn't bad enough, now it's dinner with a sick man. Daniel tells me you haven't had much chance to see our country.

Fiona Occupational hazard – leaping in and out of jeeps. Never really looking where you're going. That's why this is so nice. Thank you.

They sit in silence. Fiona sips her drink. Muturi picks up the radio and flicks stations. Some foreign pop comes on.

Muturi You like music, all kinds?

Fiona Most.

Muturi I go everywhere with this radio. When I used to work, when I could work, I'd take it with me. This thing sat next to me for twenty years, playing everything, all things, all day. People got sick of me.

Fiona What work were you in?

Muturi Factory work, nothing too hard.

Daniel It was hard, it was hard work.

Muturi But it wasn't too hard, it was gentle enough, but even that got too much in the end.

Fiona looks at him, and he feels the need to explain.

It's iron. Not enough iron in the blood. You feel weak and tired without iron, so you work slower. I tried but . . . My manager did a calculation, said I did six and half hours a week less work than the man next to me, so they let me go.

Fiona That's terrible.

Muturi No, it isn't. I'd have done the same.

Fiona And do you take supplements? Pills?

Muturi I won't take those things.

Daniel They're expensive.

Muturi I wouldn't take them anyway.

Fiona Why?

Muturi stands and shakes his head, he seems more serious now.

Muturi I'll check on dinner.

Daniel I'll go, Papa.

Muturi You stay. Excuse me.

Muturi walks out. Daniel watches him.

Fiona I didn't offend him did I?

Daniel No. He says he wouldn't take the supplements but he would, he's just convinced himself he wouldn't because that way he isn't going without. He isn't reliant on something he can't get. Do you see?

Fiona nods. Daniel sits and watches her.

Most drugs, basics, they're expensive and hard to get . . . But maybe not for much longer.
  What happens now? Will you go to the Electoral Committee?

Fiona Tomorrow.

Daniel What will you say?

Fiona That the registration was a mess. That we can help them register more people before the next round. Simply that.

Daniel What will they say?

Fiona What would you say?

Daniel goes quiet for a moment. Fiona is surprised.

Daniel You're sure about this?

Fiona It's perfectly legal.

Daniel That's not what I asked. I asked if you're sure.

Pause. They look at each other for a moment. Daniel listens to the music.

Will you need me?

Fiona Yes.

Daniel Then I'll be there.
  Do you like Elton John?

Fiona This isn't Elton John.

Daniel I know. But do you like Elton John?

Fiona (*smiling*) To an extent.

Daniel I am called Daniel because of the song. (*He sings.*) 'Looks like Daniel, must be the clouds in my eyes.' It must have been on the radio that day.

Fiona What will you do, when we're gone? When the mission is over?

Daniel Mission?

Fiona The election, I mean. It's only a couple of weeks and we'll be gone and you can get back – to what, though? What will you get back to?

Daniel Study. I want to set up a business.

Fiona Doing what?

Daniel Making money. Took me six years to finish my last two years of school. I had to work some, to help my father. My mother died. The school closed and reopened and closed and so I found another one. I want to use everything I know, somehow. What about you?

Fiona Somewhere else. Another one of these.

Daniel Another mini-bar?

Fiona In another identical hotel room. Yes, pretty much.

Daniel No time at home?

Fiona A little, but . . .

Daniel Yes?

Fiona I'm not someone who relaxes back into that life very easily.

Muturi enters carrying a basket of flat bread and a bottle of wine. He is walking with difficulty. Daniel jumps up, takes the bottle and tries to take the basket.

Muturi Let me do something. This is bread we made. And this . . . (*He takes the bottle.*) Nkwu. Forget your gin. This is homemade, palm wine. From the sap of the raffia tree. I'll go back and get the plates.

Daniel Let me help you.

Muturi I'm fine.

Daniel You'll have to make three journeys.

Muturi So, I'll make three journeys. (*He looks at Fiona.*) Try the bread.

Fiona I will. Thank you.

Muturi walks away and stops. He seems a little breathless. Daniel watches him and he spots it out the corner of his eye.

Muturi Le nga ina nwu Gordon's gin and tonic nna gi na wu ohu gi. [*Look at you, sipping your Gordon's gin and tonic while your old man waits on you hand and foot.*]

Daniel laughs as his father exits. Fiona has not understood this exchange.

Fiona What?

Daniel He was joking, about doing all the work. He would have said it in English, but he can't seem to joke in English, only be serious.

Fiona I know that feeling. We should help –

Daniel He'd hate us to. He loves this. Don't worry. How long do you have?

Fiona I don't know. I shouldn't leave it that long before I head back. I'm borrowing the driver from Henrik and I have some work to do before tomorrow.

Daniel Of course. Can I ask you something, then, in case we run out of time and I never get the chance to say it?

Fiona Of course.

Daniel switches off the radio. There is a moment of silence, Fiona realises he is serious.

Daniel Before . . . before this job . . . What I really mean is . . . What makes a person do this job for so many years? Leave home?

Fiona Do you know where Leeds is?

Daniel looks blank.

I worked for Leeds City Council. As an Election Officer. Assistant Registration and Elections Officer, actually. I was responsible amongst other things for the registration of voters.

Daniel Like you're trying to do now?

Fiona It's part of what I do now, but it's different, where I come from . . . People don't really want to vote.

Daniel No one?

Fiona Some do. But we're used to it. Bored of it. Nothing changes.

Daniel You wanted to make a change?

Fiona I wanted to register people who wanted to vote. Who want to do something with their vote. In the end, at home, it's a paperwork competition. A race between colleagues. Quotas, targets.

Daniel seems unsure. Fiona moves closer and breaks off a piece of bread.

What I mean is, you're registering people but not actual voters, because most of them just won't bother to turn up on the day and in your heart of hearts you know that they won't.

Daniel Why won't they?

Fiona We don't have the contrasts that you have here. Two very different men, very different ideas of what the future might be. Here, other places I've been . . . if you register people in a first-time election – they use it. It's like you're putting a voting slip in their hand and they didn't have it there before. It's power actually in their hands.

Daniel You like the way it makes you feel?

Fiona What's wrong with that? And even if we don't register, even if we're just brought in to observe, then at least you get to observe something changing right in front of you.

Daniel So you do want to make a change?

Fiona A difference. They're not the same thing.

Daniel And when we get bored of being able to vote, bored like Leeds, then we know we are truly democratic?

Fiona Something like that . . .

*Fiona smiles and eats some bread as Muturi
re-enters with another plate of food. He sets it
down on the table when we hear a car horn and
then see the flash of two headlights from outside.*

That's my driver.

Muturi Wait here.

Muturi instinctively moves to go outside. He exits.

Fiona He's hungry, or bored possibly?

Daniel It must be lonely . . . for you, I mean.

*Daniel and Fiona look at one another. A series of
complex emotions are bound up in these few
moments.*

I'm glad you came tonight.

Suddenly Muturi enters.

Muturi You shouldn't have switched the radio off.
Onwere accident mere. Gwongworo bu oha nmadu ndi
opposition ka ha chupuru n'okpo uzo. Ya otugharia.
Amabe ma nmadu o meruru ahu. Ha na emechi uzo.
O kwesiri ila. [*There's been an accident. A truck
carrying people canvassing for the opposition was
run off the road. It turned over. They don't know if
anyone is hurt. They're closing the road. She should
go.*]

Fiona doesn't understand.

Daniel How many people?

Muturi Thirty. (*To Fiona.*) There's been an accident
on the highway you drove in on. A truck carrying
people canvassing for the opposition . . . They shot at

the tyres and it hit a ditch and rolled over. They don't know if anyone is hurt. They're closing the road.

Daniel You should go.

Muturi You'll pass by it on your way back to the hotel. You'll see it with your own eyes. I'm tempted to go and look at it myself.

Daniel Why?

Muturi Blood is a hopeful sign. It means they're panicking. It means the President is scared he might lose. The right man has to win here – I know you understand that.

Fiona (*horrified*) Thirty . . .?

Muturi Finish your drink. Time to hold your nerve.

Suddenly on screen a truck, with headlights beaming, surges forward towards us. We hear a furious screech of brakes before a blackout.

Act Two

ONE

Saunders faces us and looks agitated.

Saunders To be honest, I'm getting royally chuffed off. Fiona Russell is now heading this observation mission in all but name. However, intercepted phone messages from her hotel room and emails from her personal account have generated no new pertinent information. She hasn't called her husband in days and I am still awaiting clearance from you to make some sort of contact with her. The phrase 'pissing in the wind' comes to mind. I mean, does anyone actually read these bloody reports I keep sending? Or is there something you're not telling me? A change in policy out here, perhaps? May I remind you I'm supposed to be your eyes and ears, so if there's something you know that I don't . . .

(*Regaining his composure.*) This morning she rose and left her hotel at 7.04 a.m. She travelled straight to a town hall in the city with her translator. She'd come for the electoral archive there and emerged barely an hour later with a cardboard box in her hand containing . . . I don't know what. I have no official access to that building, unlike her. My guess would be this is some kind of documentation to present to the Electoral Committee. But may I strongly suggest that, having no clear idea of her objective, contact should be made with Fiona Russell. And if not with her, then with a member of her team.

Unless I hear from you I'll assume you're happy for
me to go ahead and establish communication.

Sincerely, Saunders.

TWO

THIRTEEN DAYS UNTIL
THE SECOND ROUND OF VOTING

*The Central Electoral Committee. A council of three
people – Dr Daramy, Mr Sesay and a Chair, Madam
Conteh – sit and watch as Fiona steps up to a table
and a microphone.*

*A Policeman stands guard in the background while
a stenographer prepares her machine. When the session
begins the minutes will appear in Igbo on the screen
behind.*

*Daniel enters and hovers next to Fiona, holding a
box file as she prepares her notes.*

*The Policeman steps forward and sternly whispers
something to Daniel. Daniel, looking a little uneasy,
turns and whispers something in Fiona's ear. She looks
up, surprised, as he is escorted from the chamber
by the Policeman. There is a pause. Fiona is unsure
of the protocol. She leans forward towards the
microphone.*

Fiona I've just been informed that I'm not permitted
to bring my own translator into the chamber with me.

No one answers. Silence. She looks around.

Is there anyone here who would . . . ? Onwere onye
n'asu fu English? [*Does anyone here speak English?*]

Madam Conteh No one will translate because we all understand you.

How is your room?

Fiona I'm sorry?

Madam Conteh Your hotel?

Fiona My room is fine, thank you.

Madam Conteh There is a fruit platter on the menu. It's quite famous to that hotel. You can order it day or night.

Fiona Yes, I've had it.

The Policeman re-enters and takes his position. Pause.

It's a beautiful country . . . Your country. It's beautiful.

Madam Conteh There's always a pressure to say that, isn't there?

Fiona I wouldn't say it if I didn't mean it. I've travelled a lot, to some awful places.

Madam Conteh We know. And now here you are. We are senior judges, each of us.

Fiona Yes.

Madam Conteh We are used to applying the law. We've helped build this country with the decisions we've taken. Binding, difficult decisions. For the record . . . who are you?

Fiona I am the Deputy Chief of the International Election Observation Mission.

Madam Conteh You were nominated to speak to us?

Fiona Yes. I was.

Madam Conteh It's unusual for your organisation to do this?

Fiona Perhaps, but it's perfectly legal. You don't have to do anything that we recommend.

Madam Conteh We know.

Fiona But obviously we would recommend that you do.

Madam Conteh Obviously . . .

Fiona Maybe I should just . . . start?

Madam Conteh As a rule, the invitation to a session of this Committee, together with the proposed agenda, shall be sent to members of the Committee and their deputies in written form, at the latest, two days before the date set for the holding of the session.

Fiona I couldn't do that.

Madam Conteh Exceptionally, the invitation to a session of the Committee, together with the proposed agenda, may be sent at shorter notice. The Chair of the Committee shall then be obliged to explain this action at the beginning of the session – which is what I'm doing right now.

Fiona Thank you.

Madam Conteh We know why you're here.

Fiona Democracy is . . .

Fiona dries up. She looks at all the faces around her and changes tack.

We want to work with you . . . to register more voters. You have an Article 32, which makes provision for the registering of voters prior to elections. That's plural 's'. The extra registration can be got under way within days and could boost voter turnout for the second round of the Presidential campaign, which I understand to be part of your remit as the Electoral Committee.

Madam Conteh It is.

Fiona Okay. (*Taking a breath.*) Well then, next, let me start to explain how we might –

Mr Sesay In your preliminary report, that is at your press conference after the first ballot, you praised our work.

Fiona We meant that.

Mr Sesay You didn't do it in anticipation of your visit here today?

Fiona No. There have been huge strides taken in this election, but also things that I know we would not want to see happen in the next round.

Mr Sesay What things?

Fiona People being coerced. (*She looks around at them.*) I think we all know there was coercion. In many different forms.

Dr Daramy Name it.

Fiona I'm sorry?

Dr Daramy Name it. Name one act of coercion . . .

Fiona Well, for example, an article by the main opposition leader had its title changed without prior notification. (*Looking down at her notes.*) 'The Basis of All Problems – Tremendous Concentration of Power and Authority in the Hands of the President' became 'The Country needs Modernisation'.

Dr Daramy It's snappier.

Fiona Yes, perhaps, but –

Dr Daramy That's it? That is your example?

Fiona (*strong*) There are more vivid examples, some involving physical force – students being beaten, unauthorised persons being present in eleven per cent of the polling stations we visited . . . but I thought it might be best not to get too emotive about things.

Mr Sesay None of this was a part of your preliminary report.

Fiona Certain things are tolerated the first time a country tastes democracy.

Dr Daramy So why bring it up now? To try and influence us?

Fiona No. Absolutely not. Please don't misunderstand me. I'm trying to help strengthen the mandate of whoever wins. So incidents like the ones my team have observed don't take on an undue weight in the eyes of the world.

Dr Daramy They wouldn't have any weight at all if you didn't report them.

Madam Conteh Please! (*Moderating.*) What are you offering?

Fiona Support. To help explain the registration procedure to people. To help mobilise a group to assist you in the registration of more voters. Simply that. May I . . . approach you?

Madam Conteh nods. Fiona steps away from the microphone and hands out three sets of documents. Then she steps back to the mic and picks up her own set. The Committe members leaf through the document while she speaks.

Principally, we are talking about four districts. Divided into eighteen catchment areas. With one registration team per two catchment areas.

Madam Conteh This is a very large area. Do you have enough people to help register?

Fiona I think so, and in the thirteen days we have until –

Dr Daramy Nine.

Fiona I'm sorry?

Madam Conteh Nine days. The register will close four days before the second round, to be collated.

Fiona (*angry at her own mistake*) Of course. Nine days.

Mr Sesay How many people can you register, in that time?

Fiona I honestly don't know. It could take four minutes per registration, it could take fifteen.

Dr Daramy And where are the areas geographically?

Fiona Based on a rudimentary census from your electoral archive, there are huge swathes of people in the north and in the mountainous inland regions who are not registered.

Dr Daramy And this is based on . . . your research?

Fiona We want more people to vote. It's in the interests of the country, for the whole of the country, to be best represented.

Mr Sesay gestures to the stenographer, who suddenly stops typing.

Mr Sesay Allow me to be blunt. The international community would have a better time of things if the President did not win this election. Isn't that what this is about?

Fiona Absolutely not. We are here to do our job.

Mr Sesay You want to help us?

Fiona We're here to do that.

Mr Sesay You've been observing us?

Fiona That's why we've been here.

Mr Sesay Now you want to go from observing us to helping us register voters? You can understand my confusion.

Fiona Our organisation handles both remits. We offered you assistance with your registration after our first visit, before the election. You declined.

Dr Daramy Which was our right.

Fiona Of course. But your registration forms are hard to follow, notwithstanding the . . . unconventional decisions that were made with boundary lines.

Mr Sesay We've done our best.

Fiona I realise that, and I take no pleasure in telling you this, but . . . but there are elements of your work that have proved to be unconstructive to the electoral process.

Dr Daramy We've made a mess of things. Isn't that what you mean?

Fiona doesn't answer. The Committee look at one another as the stenographer's hands hover over her keyboard again.
Pause. Madam Conteh nods. As Fiona speaks, the stenographer resumes typing.

Fiona I visited an archive –

Madam Conteh We know.

Fiona This morning, I visited an archive to look at your voting records. There are massive inaccuracies in voter lists, which are confirmed by our own observations. People that had applied to be included as voters were unable to find themselves on the list on Election Day.

Mr Sesay They must not have filed the proper application documents.

Fiona Sure, but –

Mr Sesay We must have the proper documentation.

Fiona I agree, of course.

Dr Daramy Then what is your problem?

Fiona A greater effort could have been made to enfranchise those people. We could have helped you with that. We still can if you would let us.

I really think you should let us.

The Committee sit in silence. Fiona knows they still need convincing.

Two months ago, a staff member from one of the opposition parties discovered a police officer video-taping in front of their recruitment offices. The tape was marked with the date and with the initials of the party being watched. This case was taken to court with a claim against the relevant Department of Interior.

Mr Sesay I tried that case.

Fiona Yes, sir, I know. The tape appeared to be a clear case of unlawful surveillance, but even so the court upheld the argument that the police officer just happened to be 'testing' the equipment.

It's things like that which, if we're not careful, send out a worrying signal about your impartiality.

Mr Sesay stares rigidly back at Fiona.

Mr Sesay I studied at Harvard University, then ran my own legal practice for twenty-eight years. I've worked all over the world, so I'm more than happy to debate a point of law . . . but you were not present in that courtroom.

Fiona No, sir, I wasn't but –

Mr Sesay What would happen, I wonder, if we trawled through your country's recent legal history, looking for what *I* considered to be mockeries of the law? I wonder how stupid you could be made to look?

Fiona I'm not trying to make you look stupid – but this is a fragile moment for your country, and things like this are understandably amplified in this environment.

Dr Daramy (*angered*) You came here a year ago.

Fiona Not me.

Dr Daramy Your people did. You deemed us ready for democratic elections.

Fiona We did.

Dr Daramy If we are ready for democratic elections why are we not ready to register voters and oversee the elections ourselves?

Fiona This process gets observed all over the world. My country included. Genuine democratic elections are –

Dr Daramy Why say genuine? Surely if an election is democratic it is genuine implicitly?

Fiona Not always. Genuine democratic elections are hard. Sometimes they are even a bloody business.

Dr Daramy Elee eshi ohuru blood n'ime obodo ya? Owu mgbe ha lu ga civil war? Owu 500 years? Ka oforo? [*And when was the last time she saw blood in her own country? Civil war? Five hundred years? More?*]

Fiona (*unable to follow them*) I'm sorry I don't understand you.

Dr Daramy Bloody business! Elee ihe oma gbasara blood? [*What does she know of blood?*]

Madam Conteh We should return to why we're here.

Dr Daramy Gwa ya ihe mere na town hall mgbe o biara ichoputa ihe were fuo osiso. [*Tell her what happened at the town hall which she marched into, ransacked for information and promptly left.*]

Fiona I'm afraid I'll need to ask for a translator if you insist on speaking –

Dr Daramy We invited you into our country. Not the other way around. There was a need for this election. We all felt it. And yet I wonder why are we doing this? What is the point, if it means we are spoken to this way – by this . . . observer?

He stands and approaches Fiona, addressing only her.

I at least expected a lecture on economics. I half expected you to tell us how much better off we would be. The cold hard sums. But really all you're saying is that in your world democracy is inevitable, so get in line. (*With fire.*) Well, let me tell you, nothing is inevitable. And the struggle and the toil and the cost of getting here, to where we are today, to this point, has been borne by us and not by you. And yet here you are at the finish, making demands.

He turns now and speaks to the Committee, occasionally looking at Fiona.

This flat-pack democracy kit that seemed to touch down when she did – this kit that we're supposed to build and adjust as required, this is a kit of her own making, not ours. Parts of it don't fit with us, but we must accept it fully. That is the deal here whether she says so or not.

(*To Fiona.*) You do not know this country.

Obu igwe agbapuru agbapu, ma na enwere ike ichoputa ike nno n'íme ihe di otua, inwere ike ima ihe ndi ga-emebi emebi ma agbapu ya. [*It is a coiled spring and you can't begin to anticipate the energy built up inside something like that and you cannot imagine the damage that could be done if you release it.*]

Fiona It would be helpful for us to continue to speak in a language that I can understand.

Dr Daramy Your language? Yes, why not decide the fate of my country in your language?

Fiona I'm sorry but . . . Look, you were deemed ready. Our being here to observe you is an act of faith by the international community.

Dr Daramy So you tell us when we're ready? You watch us while we take our – how would you say it? Baby steps? And then you tell us in a report whether or not it is a true election.

Fiona No. The final report we publish, after the election, after everything is decided – that report is supposed to give you confidence. The simple fact we are here at all implies an overall level of faith.

Madam Conteh And suddenly we are back to 'trust'.

Fiona (*with a fight in her*) It's all we have. Elections are easy to rig. Very easy. Unless we have trust . . .

Madam Conteh I agree.

Fiona You have a rare opportunity to make this first mandate a strong historic one. The more people who vote the better it is for the country. Nationally and internationally. The more people who vote the stronger what is made will be. Your economy will be stronger. People will be more confident in investing in you. The international community will help you.

Dr Daramy Just as you're doing now?

Fiona Yes.

Pause. Dr Daramy looks around and then fixes back on Fiona.

Dr Daramy You're out of your depth. In nine days, you'll barely cover a quarter of the ground you're talking about. (*Turning back to his fellow judges.*) Let her do all the registering she wants. It won't change the result. She underestimates how much people value stability –

Madam Conteh I move to adjourn now –

Dr Daramy They've flirted with change in the first round and that's all it is, a flirtation. If a stronger mandate does even half the good that she says it will –

Madam Conteh (*more insistent*) Please. We should adjourn now –

Dr Daramy – then let her try. Let her do this. (*To the Chair.*) There. You have my recommendation.

Madam Conteh All the same, we'll adjourn and discuss this in private. (*To Fiona.*) Excuse us.

Fiona watches as the Committee and staff leave the chamber. She looks restless, concerned she hasn't done enough to convince them. After a moment she kneels and starts packing up her paperwork. Daniel re-enters and watches her.

Daniel It's over?

Fiona They're conferring. Deciding, I don't know. I think we're about to find out.

Daniel You think they'll say no? How many could you register, before the next round?

Fiona I honestly don't know. If they say yes, we can start sending people in with the literature today and we'll just keep registering until the next round. We have nine days.

Daniel I thought it was thirteen?

Fiona I was wrong.

Daniel But you can't cover the towns and the rural areas in nine days though, can you? Not evenly, I mean.

Fiona No.

Daniel But it has to be an even effort, doesn't it?

Fiona Does it?

Daniel and Fiona exchange a look which is quickly interrupted by Madam Conteh's re-entry.

Madam Conteh I've seen you on television.

Fiona In the corner of the screen perhaps.

Madam Conteh You look hungry.

Fiona I'm fine.

Madam Conteh glances back at the empty chamber and spots Daniel. He withdraws and she waits until she is sure he has gone.

Madam Conteh We all have strong opinions about the best way forward.

Fiona Of course.

Madam Conteh I don't expect you to understand how strange things suddenly seem. This is a different view of the world. Your view. We're still adjusting. But we'll do this. We'll work with you. We'll try.

Fiona Thank you.

Madam Conteh Tell me, are you in touch with the military?

Fiona I've tried to get a meeting.

Madam Conteh Try harder. The President has the loyalty of the rank and file police and the army, so they ought to know exactly what is happening. There's no room for misunderstanding.

I think you should know . . . a policeman died in a protest outside the town hall today. After you left it.

Fiona's face falls. She struggles to take this in.

You did not need to ask permission from us to go there, but I wish that you had. What you did, going to the archive that way – creates a tension. People panic when they see that you have become involved. When they see that the international community has crossed a line.

Fiona (*defensive*) We had every right to be there.

Madam Conteh You were trying to build a case by being there. I just hope you've thought this through. Whatever you have started here . . . I hope you know how it might end.

Madam Conteh walks away as Fiona stands alone, looking ill, compromised and unsure.

SEVEN DAYS UNTIL THE SECOND ROUND VOTE:
REGISTRATION IS UNDER WAY

A village square. Edi and Daniel open out a folding table. Then from two rucksacks they unpack clipboards, pens and election literature. A woman, Duduzile, steps forward and watches them.

After a moment, Edi turns and realises Duduzile is staring at them, but before she is able to speak her phone suddenly starts ringing. Edi raises her hand to apologise and switches it off before looking back at the woman.

Edi Are you here to register? Good morning. Do you want to vote?

Duduzile doesn't respond and so Edi picks up a piece of paper and marks a thick cross on it. She holds it up.

We're doing this for the second round. So you can vote in time. We have teams all the way up this rise today. Up the hill. We only need very basic details.

Still Duduzile doesn't speak. Daniel notices and, grabbing a clipboard from the table, steps over to them.

Daniel Asi aga ime iha second round, ka unu nwe ike ivotu na oge. Ihe anyi choro ari hu ahua. [*We're doing* *this for the second round, so you can vote in time. We need very basic details.*]

Edi (*to Duduzile*) Just your name and address or an identification number.

Daniel Ahua gi na ebe ibi ma owu identification number. [*Just your name and address or an identification number.*]

Edi (*to Duduzile*) There'll be a polling station less than a kilometre away. Could you get there?

Daniel Onwere nga aga evotu n'eru hu gi one kilometre. Inwere ike iru ebe ahu? [*There'll be a polling station less than a kilometre away. Will you be able get there?*]

Duduzile Nwam voturu oge gara gara. Onwere oku tem tem n'eku ka ihe an'eji eme isi. [*My son voted in the first round. He has a moped that sounds like a hairdryer.*]

Daniel She says she has a son. He voted in the first round. He has a moped that sounds like a hairdryer. He would take her.

Duduzile Agaghim iju nwam kporom. Agaghim eje. [*I won't ask him to take me and I won't go.*]

Daniel But she won't ask him and she won't go.

Edi Why?

Fiona and Tony enter with boxes of registration forms as Duduzile slowly raises her finger and points straight at her. Fiona doesn't notice as she places the box down.

Duduzile Abiaram ihu ya. [*I'm here to see her.*]

Daniel (*surprised, to Fiona*) She's here to see you.

Tony Well, does she want to register?

Edi I already asked her.

Fiona (*to Duduzile*) Good morning. Do you want to vote?

Fiona steps over to her but just as she does so Duduzile quickly takes something out from under her arm. It's long, thin and wrapped in a cloth. She waves it.

Duduzile (*calling out*) Obinna!

Obinna, Duduzile's young son, enters with a badly beaten face. Fiona, Edi and Daniel are taken aback by the severity of his bruises.

Onwegi ike iga etiti ahia ji ihu ya. [*He won't go out of the square and show his face.*]

Obinna M ga aga, ujo adia atum. [*Yes I will, I'm not scared.*]

Duduzile Ha amadighi onye owu ma ha kuja saya ihu. Anum na inu n'edozi ih'unu m'asi ka unu hu ya. [*They didn't even know him but they did that to his face anyway. I heard you were here setting up and I wanted you to see him.*]

Daniel (*to Fiona*) Someone beat him and she wanted you to see.

Duduzile Obinna, tugharia. [*Obinna, turn around.*]

Obinna Agaghim itughari. [*I'm not turning around.*]

Duduzile Ji ha. Welie uwe gi elu. [*Show them. Lift up your shirt.*]

Obinna Mba, agaghim ime ya. [*I'm not lifting up my shirt.*]

Daniel She wants him to lift up his shirt but he won't.

Duduzile Agaghim ivotu. Owum gi ikwe nwa nmu vote kwa. Achorom si gi hu ya. Achorom ima ihe iga eme maka ya. [*I won't vote. And I won't let my son vote either. I wanted you to see him. I want to know what you're going to do about this.*]

Daniel (*to Fiona*) She won't vote and she won't let him vote either now. She wants to know if you can help her son.

Fiona Ask her what that is.

Fiona points at the object Duduzile is holding and she unwraps it. It's a dirty chrome wing mirror from a moped.

Duduzile Ochoro ka enye hu ya hu, mana agwalam ya na obanyele na evidence.

Daniel 'He wants it back, but I told him that it's evidence now.'

As Duduzile continues Daniel simultaneously translates for her.

Duduzile Hu ji igwe hu doturu oku tem tem ya kuo ya nihu. Ihee wu obara nwa nmuru. Aga bem isacha ya. Ma'ga na nga nde police. Ha gwam were oche. Oke oge aga, ha'sim lawa. Ya arika awum ewu nwo. Oyi amamadiam. Achorom ma gi were ya me ihe.

Daniel 'They tore it off his bike and beat him around the face with it. That's my son's blood. I haven't washed it. I've been to the police. They told me to take a seat and then two hours later they said I should go home. I felt stupid, ill with it. I want you to take it and use it.'

Tony We can't . . . we can't take it. Tell her that, Daniel.

Fiona takes the rear mirror from Duduzile. She looks at Obinna, who stands proudly in front of her.

Edi If it had anything to do with the election we could write it down. If her son would be willing to talk to us . . .

Daniel Osi owuru ma ichoro igwa anyi okwu aga ede ya ede. [*She said if he wanted to talk to us she would write it down.*]

Duduzile Ide ya ede? Ogwula? Ogwula ihe og'ime? [*Write it down? That's it? That's what she'd do?*]

Edi I know making a record of it doesn't seem like anything but –

Duduzile Gwa ya le nwam anya. [*Tell her to look at my son.*]

Daniel (*to Fiona*) She wants you to look at her son.

Obinna Mama!

Fiona looks at Obinna.

Fiona Daniel, will you ask him if he knows the men who did this –

Obinna I understand you.

Fiona Then tell me what happened.

Obinna For the first round – I ran people back and forth. One at a time, on my bike. Till they recognised me. Stopped me. Pulled off my wing mirror and beat me around the head with it. I fell on the ground. They said things.

Tony Who?

Obinna You know who . . . I mean you never know, but you know.

Edi What did they say?

Obinna 'We have taken someone's penis. A man's penis and cut it off at the base and tucked it in his pocket. We have cut eyebrows from people's faces. We'll find a way to put our hand inside you and grab a hold of something and pull at it. Pull it loose, pull it out and show it up to you.'

Fiona looks uncomfortable. Duduzile spots this.

Duduzile Elee ihe igwa ga ya? Gwa kwa ya ihe nile o. [*What are you telling her? Make sure to tell her everything.*]

Obinna looks at his mother, knowing she cannot understand him.

Obinna The second round of voting – I'll take more people. My mother doesn't want me to. She thinks I won't, but I will. I won't let them win. I'll start as early as the polling stations open and I'll drive people back and forth.

Daniel Maybe you shouldn't.

Obinna I think I have to.

Fiona I think that's very brave.

Obinna I just think I have to, that's all. I think that's all there is to it.

Fiona There's a van. I've seen it.

Obinna I know.

Duduzile (*to Daniel*) Osi nini? [*What did she say?*]

Daniel looks at Fiona, concerned at where she's going with this.

Fiona Do you know who owns it?

Obinna Yes, I know who owns it.

Duduzile Ihe a owu nini? [*What is this now?*]

Fiona It's dangerous. But it's probably less conspicuous than a motorbike. And you could take more people in a much shorter time. If you're set on going.

Obinna It's quieter than my moped, certainly.

Daniel (*with concern*) Fiona!

Fiona Look I'm sorry I can't do more. It will be recorded, what happened to your son, but I also think he's very brave.

Daniel Osi na ogara icho ime ihe karia ke omere, na oga ide ya na akwukwo, osi kwa na nwa gi nwoke nwere obi dimpka. [*She says she wishes she could do more and that it will be recorded and that she thinks your son is very brave.*]

87

Fiona Where I come from, a boy his age would hardly have the patience to take himself and queue and vote. To make time in the day to do that . . . But to take other people, those people who can't get there . . .

Daniel (*to Duduzile*) Ebem si bia – [*Where I come from* –]

Duduzile (*pointing at Obinna's face*) Ichere na obi di ihe ahu? [*You think that's brave?*]

Daniel 'Do you think that's brave?' she says.

Fiona Yes, I do.

Duduzile Iwuu nne nmadu?

Daniel 'You're not a mother, are you?'

Daniel simultaneously translates as Duduzile speaks.

Duduzile Le nwam nwoke. Amam si enweghim ike ikwusi ya. Mara, na mgbe ozo, enwere ike idotu ya otu anya ya, ma owu di ha abuo.

Daniel 'Look at my son. I know I can't stop him. But next time he'll lose an eye or maybe both.'

Duduzile (*to Daniel*) Gwa ya okwu. Ori ka inwere uche. Elee uru obara n' ino ebe e. Akpom si inwere ike ime ihe. [*You talk to him. You look like you've got some sense between your ears. What good is it you being here? I thought you could do something.*]

Daniel She thought we could do something.

Daniel looks at Fiona as she hands back the wing mirror to Duduzile.

Fiona I'm sorry . . . But your son is right. You can't let these people win. You should register to vote. Let him drive you. Walk in that polling station with your son. You'll never feel prouder. Daniel . . . tell her, please.

FOUR

TWO DAYS BEFORE
THE ELECTORAL REGISTER CLOSES

A hotel bar. Saunders stands with a gin and tonic in his hand while Daniel shifts around uneasily.

Saunders Onwe ihe m ga ewetara gi? [*Can I get you anything?*]

Daniel We're not supposed to accept gifts.

Saunders It's a drink I'm offering, not steak knives. Look, I know the rules. It's not a gift, it's hospitality.

Daniel looks around anxiously. Saunders takes a sip of his drink and watches him.

Saunders You're sweating. Your head is wet.

Daniel I don't want to be here.

Saunders Then go.

Daniel How did you get my name?

Saunders The Embassy.

Daniel Who are you?

Saunders I told you.

Daniel No you didn't – not really.

Saunders I report to the Foreign Office, Daniel. No one will recognise you. Relax. I won't keep you long. You don't have to talk to me at all.

Daniel thinks for a moment before making the decision to leave. Saunders seems genuinely surprised to see him walking away. He calls after him.

Saunders What is she doing? What does she want, Daniel? That's all I need to know. I care about this country. It's my home now, too!

Daniel stops but remains turned away from Saunders.

This massive registration effort that's under way . . . it's huge and I know how exhausted you all are, but these matters, they're of interest to us all, they shouldn't be kept private.

Daniel (*wrestling with his conscience*) Nothing is being kept private.

Saunders Then tell me.

Daniel turns. Saunders takes this as his cue to pull out a dictaphone.

Daniel No.

Saunders I've got a terrible memory and this is my second. (*Lifting his glass.*)

Daniel I said no.

Saunders sighs and tucks the dictaphone back in his pocket.

Saunders It boils down to one question really. Does she have an agenda?

Daniel . . . Of course.

Saunders And what is it?

Daniel To register fifty thousand more voters before the next round.

Saunders I know that. Why?

Daniel It's within her remit.

Saunders (*more insistent*) Why?

Daniel She doesn't like what she's seen. What she's observed since she got here.

Saunders She told you this?

Daniel I translate for her sometimes. Her words go through me.

Saunders Okay.

Daniel She doesn't like the President.

Saunders Neither do I.

Daniel For different reasons to you. You don't like him because your government can't do business with him.

Saunders That's not true.

Daniel Fine, but I know her reasons are very different to yours.

Saunders waits for him to say more. He becomes impatient.

91

Saunders And? What are they? Her reasons?

Daniel She doesn't like him for the man he is. What she's seen him do.

Saunders What about you?

Daniel I hate him, more than the both of you put together.

Saunders Yet here you are, standing, talking to me.

You're the closest person to her out here. You have better access to her than anyone. Just look me in the eye and tell me you trust her, that's all.

Daniel I trust her.

Saunders Really? I contacted three translators before you, a driver, I even tried to talk to a member of her team. I didn't tell a single one of them who I was, because I knew in an instant that they wouldn't say a word against her. But you –

Daniel I'm not sure that what she's doing is right!

As soon as this is out of his mouth Daniel feels a huge wave of relief as if it has been building up in him for some time.

But that's different to not trusting her.

Saunders You think she has your best interests at heart, the country's best interests?

Daniel Yes, I do, I think . . . (*Gathering himself.*) Look, I won't say any more. I shouldn't have said that.

Saunders Yes, you should, of course you should. And I'd like us to stay in touch.

Daniel No. We can't.

Saunders I know how hard she's driving her team. But very few of them realise the full extent of what she's doing, except perhaps you. (*As he slips his hand into his breast pocket.*) I know things are difficult for you. I asked around, I know your father can't work. Drugs are expensive. What's the condition again?

Saunders pulls out his wallet and holds it.

Daniel What is that?

Saunders My wallet. Have a look inside. It's my money. But I have nothing to spend it on. Why don't you use it? To help your father, perhaps.

Daniel stares at him. Pause.

Daniel, all I know is –

Daniel You don't know anything or I wouldn't be standing here. Foreign Office . . . Look at you! What is that? Gordon's gin and tonic? A creased linen suit and a cheap wallet you bought outside the airport when you first came. Foreign Office. Could you be any more foreign? No. You don't know anything.

Saunders I know about Michael Russell. Her husband, back home. But I'm sure she's told you all about him too. She wouldn't lead you up the garden path, would she?

Daniel stares at him while he slips his wallet back into a pocket.

You two are close, I've seen that for myself, but she's using you. She has her own agenda, Daniel. And I may be foreign, but I've been here long enough to know how horrific things can get and how quickly too. Do you think she knows that, after a few weeks in this country? Stay in touch, let me know how she's getting on. That's all I ask.

Saunders exits. Daniel seems in turmoil over this conversation. Above him the lights flicker. He looks up, surprised. The lights flicker once more before going out entirely.

FIVE

ELECTION NIGHT:
SECOND-ROUND RESULT IMMINENT

Everything is in complete darkness. Suddenly we hear a voice.

Wink Hold on. Stay where you are. There's nothing to worry about. Let me assure you that I know exactly what I'm doing. This happens all the time so it's nothing to be concerned about. Nearly there now. This is the one. Okay now, here we go!

The roar of a generator suddenly brings the lights blinking back on. We are in a bar now. The smiling owner, Wink, is facing Fiona with a bottle of beer in his hand and an apron tied around his waist.

He looks at Fiona for a moment before he leans forward and kisses her on the mouth. Fiona looks back at him, a little shocked.

Wink (*delighted*) They gave me a piece of paper. I shut a curtain and took a pen and marked a cross on the paper. I put it into a metal box that was riveted. I walked outside after that and I went straight to pick up my son from school. It is a gift that you've given us.

94

Fiona No, it isn't me that's –

Wink It is. You're here. Thank you.

Fiona (*happy*) You're welcome.

Wink You always wear these clothes. I know you. From the news. You blew this fuse.

Fiona Sorry. (*Pointing.*) I was trying to turn the TV on.

Wink You can't have the TV and the fridge working at the same time. You have to make a decision, which is most important . . . always a big decision.

Wink twists off the lid of the beer and hands the bottle to Fiona.

Fiona Let's stick with the fridge for now. (*She takes a sip.*)

Wink You are waiting for the announcement?

Fiona For a phone call.

Wink You'll know first?

Fiona Yes.

Wink Before the television knows?

Fiona Yes.

Wink I have heard nothing. (*Nodding at the TV.*) No one is saying a word. If anyone knew it would be my brother-in-law. He works for a paper. The sports pages, but he would know.

Fiona It takes time to filter through.

Wink But you will know the result first?

Fiona Yes . . .

Wink Can I get my wife? When your phone rings?

Fiona Okay.

Wink (*smiling*) My mother pretended to be blind. She took dark glasses and a stick to the polling station and asked them to help her into the booth. She told them who she wanted to vote for because she was convinced that they would put the cross next to someone else's name. My mother is suspicious. But they didn't. They let her have her choice. She couldn't believe it.

Fiona (*enjoying this conversation*) What will change, do you think?

Wink Everything.

Fiona Why?

Wink No matter who wins. We have a choice. It is our choice.

Fiona And what if you lose, if your choice comes second?

Wink It was still my choice.

Fiona You would support either man?

Wink I would try.

Tony walks in, wiping his hands on his trousers.

Tony No lock on the toilet. Had to hold it while I went. Then the lights went out. Fucking lunacy. (*To Wink.*) Beer, please? (*To Fiona.*) How do you say beer?

Fiona Beer.

Tony (*to Wink*) Beer, please.

Wink nods and hands him a beer. Tony has a sip and spots the TV set.

Tony TV no good?

Fiona They'll call. We'll know first.

Tony I feel a bit cut off.

Fiona We've got four mobile phones between us.

Tony (*restless*) I just want to know now. I can't understand why you didn't want to wait at the office?

Fiona I wanted to hear about it somewhere like this.

Tony Romantic, aren't you?

Fiona looks around, Tony watches her.

You expecting someone?

Fiona No I just thought . . . my translator.

Tony Young guy?

Fiona Daniel. I wonder where he's watching it, that's all.

Wink watches Tony as he takes a sip and then surreptitiously checks his mobile phone – no calls. A pause.

Tony So . . . Did you vote?

Wink Yes.

Tony Good man. And your neighbours?

Wink Yes.

Tony Very good. Here's to you, then.

*Tony takes another slug just as one of Fiona's
phones ring. Her second phone also rings. Both
phones in Tony's pocket suddenly trill into life as
well. Wink runs off shouting.*

Wink Waletta! Waletta! Ha na-acho ikpo result. Anyi
nwere onye ma ihe mega ebe. Nwanyi, ichoro inu
onye meriri ka o ow' ichohu? [*They are about to
announce this result. We have someone in the know
here. Woman, do you want to hear who won this
thing or not?*]

*Fiona picks up one of the phones, so does Tony.
The other two fall silent.*

Fiona Tell me . . .

*They both listen and wait before a smile spreads
slowly across Fiona's face. She grabs Tony and they
start hugging, but in complete silence.*
   *Then, still with the phone pressed to her ear, Fiona
hears something which makes her break away. Her
face falls. They both listen for a moment longer,
and then start speaking hurriedly into their mobiles.*

Fiona They can't do this.

Tony No statement yet?

Fiona No specifics? Okay. Can I suggest? No, listen,
can I suggest . . .

Tony Which channel? Hold on.

*Tony reaches forward to switch the TV on. The
lights cut out.*

Oh come on!

Wink Hold on. Nobody move. Nothing serious has occurred here. Drink your beer and everything will be back to normal before you even know it.

The roar of a generator brings the lights blinking back on once again. This time it is Wink's wife, Waletta, who is standing a few feet away from Fiona. The women look at one another for a moment as Fiona hangs on the line, while Tony continues to talk into his phone.

Tony We'll head back, so pull everyone together. We'll need copies of the statement they released, that's the first thing . . .

Wink comes in and joins his wife.

Fiona We're on our way.

They look at her, full of expectation.

Waletta Please? Tell us . . . Who is our President?

Fiona looks almost punch drunk. She hangs up and slides her phone away.

Fiona There is a protocol. When somebody wins, your Electoral Committee is supposed to announce it. The Chairwoman is supposed to . . .

Wink (*with anticipation*) And when will she do that?

Fiona She's been arrested, on corruption . . . on charges of . . .

Waletta So who'll announce it?

Tony (*coming off his phone*) Can you believe this house-arrest bullshit? I mean what the hell is going on here?

Fiona Without her they can't announce the result.

Tony But that doesn't change anything. It doesn't change the outcome, I mean.

Fiona If they don't announce the result there is no outcome. They're trying to steal it back.

Tony Maybe they're stalling. I mean, maybe they want something.

Waletta Please, who will announce the result?

Fiona's mind is racing now, as she tries to stay in front of the events.

Fiona Perhaps *we* could.

Tony You know we can't do that.

Fiona Look, if no one says anything it suddenly looks shaky. And that isn't fair or safe.

Tony Fiona, there's a protocol to follow.

Fiona You know what it's like out there, you can feel it. Any uncertainty –

Tony We don't speak till the decision is made public.

Fiona Sure.

Tony We don't announce it to the world.

Fiona Sure, I know.

Tony That's not our job.

Fiona Tony, I said I know! But the Electoral Committee obviously aren't saying anything.

Tony It's their election. We can't suddenly tell people who we think won it.

Waletta Why can't we know?

Waletta looks from Tony to Fiona, waiting to hear more. Neither of them speaks.

You just said it was our election. You said that for yourself. Why can't we know now?

Fiona I'm sorry . . . There's a protocol.

Tony We should go back.

Tony's phone rings again and he answers it, stepping to one side.

Yeah, we're on our way – what? Say again . . . You're breaking up, I can't hear you . . .

Wink We don't know who has won, then?

Fiona Yes, we know who has won. The leader of the opposition. By sixteen thousand votes.

Waletta and Wink look at one another. Fiona senses something.

You didn't vote for him?

Wink I did. My wife didn't, and she's the one who understands it all, I must admit.

Waletta He is an unknown quantity and he has no religion. He will sell out our country and our resources and call it taking our rightful place in the world.

Fiona I think you're wrong. He's a good man.

Waletta You know him?

Fiona No, but –

Waletta To start with they are all good men. You wait till he has the army and the police in his pocket. You see how good he is then.

   If he won, I said I would try and support him and I will. Even though, for me, he's weak and not ready to govern. Still, *you* must announce he has won. (*To Wink.*) Tell her.

Wink We'll listen to you. Tell us on television.

Fiona We can't. That's not the way we do things. After it's official then my organisation will speak.

Fiona hands back her beer and offers Wink some coins but he won't accept them.

Waletta Make it strong and certain, whatever happens.

Tony Fiona . . .

Waletta Don't leave us not knowing which way to look. That's all we ask.

Tony Fiona . . .

Tony holds out his phone, gingerly. Fiona turns and looks at him.

Fiona I'll call them back.

Tony I really think you'll want to take this.

Fiona Who is it?

Tony The Head of the Military.

SIX

Saunders looks distracted and uncomfortable.

Saunders Look, I've been seeing a woman out here, a teacher, for some time. She's a friend and . . . it's company more than anything. The point is she called me up, frantic. She closed her school but only for half a day. She felt it important to mark the occasion, for the children. A democratically elected President. The next day a brick came through her window and then another. They said she closed the school because she was a supporter of the opposition.

We still await the official declaration of who won the second round but there's no new chair of the Electoral Committee to announce it. In the vacuum created there is inevitable violence but it's getting worse. The division between those wanting to embrace the new and those clinging on to what was is vast. The only thing they share in common are the tools they use – bricks and bats to make their point.

(*With bitterness.*) Thank you for your correspondence, at last. I shouldn't have doubted that you were aware of the situation out here, I just think you could have . . . could have told me what you had in mind a little sooner. If you're confident in things proceeding this way then I'll back off from Fiona Russell, as per your instructions.

My friend, she asked me how long would it take. This bloodletting. All I could say was it's a part of the process. Still, she's trying to teach these kids in the midst of all this and no one wants to learn, so they spend the day looking out of the window to see what's coming next.

A car bomb goes off, triggering several alarms and the sound of falling cement dust and broken glass.

SEVEN

TWO DAYS AFTER THE SECOND ROUND: THE PRESIDENT HAS NOT CONCEDED

A restaurant. Fiona enters looking for someone. Chimma, a waitress, spots her.

Chimma A table, ma'am?

Fiona I'm looking for someone.

Chimma There was a fight in here. People moved into the bar while we cleaned it up.

Fiona What happened?

Chimma I don't know. A businessman and another man. One of them threw a bread roll because the other one was talking too loudly about the President, on purpose so everyone could hear.

Fiona Criticising him?

Chimma Praising him to the heavens. They rolled around for a while, got sweaty and gave up. Then we threw them out. Their wives kept on eating. It's happening more and more. Shame, one of them is a regular too. Losing his head that way. It's embarrassing.

Behind Fiona, Declan shows a woman to his table. He sits and takes a drag on a cigarette. Fiona takes a deep breath and steps towards him.

Fiona Declan.

Declan Fiona. Can you believe this? I'm smoking in a fucking restaurant. Isn't that marvellous? I mean, not prowling around outside under some bloody awning, but actually, you know, smoking. Do you want one?

Fiona Declan, I –

Declan Have a seat. Join us.

Fiona Declan, can we talk?

Declan This is Judy, my producer slash camerawoman.

Fiona Hi.

Judy Hello.

Declan Just the one paycheque, though.

Judy Sadly.

Declan Fucking BBC. Fiona, sit. Eat something, smoke. Let's enjoy a bit of bloody civilisation here. Our last night! Can you believe it? I could kiss the fucking waiters, you know. Very excited. Eat something, I'll pay.

Judy Wow!

Declan I know, wow, right? A measure of my excitement. Home, Fiona.

Fiona Declan, I need to ask you a favour.

Declan Should I put my work face on?

Fiona Yes, you should.

Fiona looks serious. Declan suddenly takes her in and then stubs out his cigarette. Fiona sits. This is difficult for her. She looks up at Judy.

Declan You don't have to worry about Judy. She's an old hand at all this, just like you. A veteran. They sent her out here when this bloody thing went to a second round.

Judy (*to Fiona*) We were actually in Cambodia together.

Fiona Were we?

Judy I was running a crew out there. You were working for an observation team.

Declan Still is.

Judy You probably don't remember.

Fiona I'm sorry, I –

Judy It was a little bit tamer than this.

Fiona Yes.

Judy We never met properly. I always thought you looked very –

Declan Intense? Tightly wound?

Judy Busy.

Declan That's a better word.

Judy looks at Fiona and feels some sympathy for her. She can tell she's struggling with something.

Judy Tell you what – I'll leave you to it.

Declan You don't have to –

Judy It's fine. Safe journey home, Fiona.

Fiona Thank you.

Judy stands and walks away. Declan half rises and watches her go.

Declan Bollocks . . . It's taken me all bloody week to get her to say yes to dinner. I'm so fucking lonely. Aren't you lonely? I mean, Christ. Home, Fiona. Home. A result.

Fiona But no announcement.

Declan It'll come.

Fiona I'm not so sure.

She looks up at him and he falls silent.

Declan What?

Fiona This is confidential.

Declan Of course.

Fiona I mean it, Declan.

Declan I'll uncross my fingers.

Fiona I had a phone call, from the head of the military. Two days ago.

Declan You?

Declan explodes into laughter.

Fiona Will you listen to me?

Declan falls silent.

We requested a meeting when we first got here. We always do. With the military and the police. It's part of protocol during an election, but they never scheduled anything. Now they have. I've been asked to meet –

Declan With the head of the fucking military. Why?

Fiona It has something to do with the result, I'm sure of it. They're stalling, they must want something.

Declan What?

Fiona I don't know. But it didn't come through the usual channels. Look, don't fly home tonight.

Declan Is this some sort of bloody joke?

Fiona Stay one more day. Two more.

Declan My job is done. So is yours.

She pulls her chair in closer.

Fiona Let me meet with him, find out what they want. If it appears that they're ready to concede . . . I'll tell you.

Declan So?

Fiona On camera . . .

Declan You'd do that?

Fiona If they don't seem to be even considering it . . . if they're just playing for time, then I'll make a statement to you before I call a press conference. I'll tell people the election was free and fair and that the opposition leader won. I'll say they're trying to steal this election.

Declan (*suddenly stubbing out his cigarette*) I'm gonna go and pack, for home. I suggest you do the same.

He stands and signals for the bill.

Fiona I've watched your reports online. Tonight's was awful.

Declan Harrowing, you mean?

Fiona No – shit, Declan, is what I mean. This administration is beating people – where are the images, where are the eyewitness reports? Do a piece on, on the violence. That bus that was shot up and run off the road.

Declan That was two weeks ago.

Fiona The car bombs. The things I've observed.

Declan Fee . . . this election is small beer. Bottom line. Not only that, but there's a perception that it was free and fair. You said so yourself. A lot of ugly little things were tidied away at your organisation's behest. I'm not stupid, I read your first-round report – I know most of the stuff that was left out. I also know the arguments. Big picture, right? You're not here to rock the boat. You're all about providing solid foundations, that's what you do. Well, fine, but you can't suddenly change the rules now.

Fiona Why not? They have.

Declan It's their game, Fiona, not yours. What's wrong with you?

Chimma arrives at the table and places the bill down before stepping discreetly away. Declan picks it up but looks at Fiona and finds himself hesitating.

Christ . . .
Alright. I'll stay.

Fiona Thank you.

Declan One more day . . . but as a journalist. And if you go on camera, it'll cost you your job. That last part I say as a friend.

EIGHT

THREE DAYS AFTER THE SECOND ROUND: THE PRESIDENT HAS STILL NOT CONCEDED

A beautiful garden. Daniel steps forward dressed in a suit, waiting. Fiona enters, wearing a jacket now. She's pleased to see him, but Daniel is harder to read.

Fiona Am I late?

Daniel A little.

Fiona You look very smart . . . Are you ready for this? I think the less we say the better. Let's just hear him out, let him do all the talking. One of my hands is shaking. You look very smart.

Daniel You said that.

Fiona You look very calm too.

Daniel Only on the outside.

Fiona I'm glad it's you . . . Where have you been? Every time I go to the pool to grab a translator you're not there.

Daniel My father got worse – that's why I . . .

Fiona Oh, I'm sorry. I hope he's feeling –

Daniel He passed away last night.

Fiona is speechless. Daniel seems lost. They look at one another for a moment.

Fiona Daniel . . . I'm so sorry.

Daniel When are you leaving?

Fiona I don't know. Soon.

Daniel If you're still here will you come to the funeral?

Fiona Of course.

Suddenly, a soldier in combat fatigues marches in, halts, and stamps his feet to attention. Fiona looks at him. A well-decorated General, Okute, enters. He looks calm and smiles. He points at a bedding plant.

General Okute That one?

Daniel Oleaster.

General Okute And that one?

Daniel Female peony. That's cherry laurel right behind it.

General Okute Remarkable. (*To Fiona.*) We were playing this game before you arrived.

Fiona I'm sorry I was late, I –

General Okute (*waving this off and pointing at Daniel*) His mother was a gardener. Makes no difference, of course. I too am a gardener. I plant these things myself but I have no idea what they are. My wife points and I plant. Not that I mind. It's good, upending the chain of command . . . once in a while.

General Okute takes in Fiona and then looks back to Daniel.

How old are you?

Daniel Twenty-five, sir.

General Okute I was a colonel at that age. You're a success story, though, aren't you? You're progress. You're how far we've come under this President. Educated, capable. No one can say this country has failed you, now can they?

Daniel No, sir.

General Okute No, sir. Good. (*Turning back to Fiona, whose benefit this has been for.*) You may leave us now.

Fiona I'd prefer it if he stayed. To avoid confusion.

General Okute As you wish.

The General turns and salutes the guard who salutes him back and steps away. The three of them are left alone now.

I'm sorry you were snuck in the back way. I'd just rather we talked out here.

Fiona That's fine, it's a chance to see your beautiful garden.

General Okute Thank you, but that's not why I did it. I want to make it clear from the outset . . . I didn't seek this meeting. Do you understand me?

Fiona One of your staff called and –

General Okute (*firm*) You requested this meeting a month ago or more, when you first came. Correct?

Fiona That's right.

General Okute So I'm simply honouring that request now. If you are asked, I didn't seek this meeting. Is that clear?

Fiona understands what he means. She nods.

My President has a question. It's simple. Like a child's question, actually. He wants you to answer it.

Fiona Me?

General Okute Someone like you. Someone with your vantage point. His question is, what happens now?

Fiona hesitates.

Fiona Sir, I'm really not the right person to –

General Okute I'm here to negotiate.

Fiona With all due respect –

General Okute A horrible phrase.

Fiona What is there to negotiate? Your President has lost.

The General looks at Fiona sternly.

Does he concede that he's lost?

General Okute Of course.

Fiona You say of course, but he hasn't made a statement yet.

General Okute There's time for that. What happens now? That is the question.

Fiona I can't answer that.

General Okute Why not?

Fiona I have very limited authority out here, sir. Please understand –

General Okute I know all that. I know full well your position. Now please answer the question.

Fiona What exactly does he want?

General Okute Immunity . . . from any prosecution and to be able to remain in the country.

Fiona is astonished by the General's honesty, and tempted too.

Fiona I can't . . . I really can't . . . This is far above any level of influence that I –

General Okute But is it possible, do you think? In your opinion?

Fiona Yes . . . it's possible.

General Okute We need an exit strategy and you need a new Chair of the Electoral Committee to announce the result and set the wheels in motion. That person needs to be appointed by the President. And he's willing to do that as his last act in office.

Fiona My responsibility out here is –

General Okute Mrs Russell, my understanding was that you're a person who makes things happen. Well, this is your chance. You're in a good position to give advice. That's all. What happens now? Talk to me as if I were the President.

Daniel looks at Fiona. She hesitates, takes a breath and seizes the moment.

Fiona First of all there must be the appointment of a new Chair of the Committee and the announcement of the result.

General Okute It'll be done.

Fiona Then a fully published set of election figures.
Clear and transparent. A paper trail.

General Okute What else?

Fiona A reassurance that there will be no crackdown,
that people are free to celebrate the result.

General Okute Not everyone will be celebrating, you
realise. It was closer than people might care to think.
What about your report?

Fiona It's nearly finished. When the result is
announced by the Electoral Committee then we'll
deliver it.

General Okute And that will be it?

Fiona No, that will just be the start. The very
beginning of things.

General Okute My President wants to go out with
dignity.

Fiona If he does these things and quickly, I'm sure
he'll be greatly respected for it.

*The General thinks about this and then holds out
his hand. Fiona hesitates before accepting it. They
shake. Daniel watches.*

General Okute Life is about to change.

Daniel Immeasurably.

*Fiona and the General both look at Daniel. The
young man's face is full of doubt.*

General Okute So look pleased, why don't you? I
would be, perhaps, if I could see a place for myself in

all this. (*To Daniel.*) Are you pleased? You didn't answer me.

Daniel looks at him. Fiona looks at Daniel. There is a moment of silence in which Daniel says nothing. General Okute understands.

Or maybe you did. What a skilled communicator you are.

I'll talk to the former President. Funny, that's the first time I've called him that.

Fiona And he'll listen to you?

General Okute I advise him. And I know that other people will say what you have said. He'll hear it sooner or later, so it might as well be from me.

Fiona Thank you.

General Okute No, thank you. For your frankness. (*Nodding at Daniel.*) You two are well matched.

Someone will escort you out, but may I ask you a courtesy? To leave the same way you came in? I hope you don't think that's rude.

Fiona Of course not, but I don't really understand.

General Okute I'd rather no one knew we'd met. If you were working for me I would have you watched. My guess is your government is doing just that.

Fiona smiles incredulously.

Fiona I think I can assure you I'm not being watched.

General Okute No?

Fiona No. I'm just an observer here.

General Okute Come now, Mrs Russell, there's no such thing. That's rather like saying a knife is just something to carry in your pocket. Don't worry. It's for my protection, not for yours. You'll be fine.

Fiona Why do you say that?

General Okute If you worked for me and I didn't like how you were conducting yourself I would have stopped you long before now.

He looks back up into the sky.

Looks like rain. He'll have to make his concession speech inside. He won't like that.

General Okute exits. Fiona noticeably exhales and seems a little stunned.

Fiona It's over.

Daniel What are you doing?

Fiona What?

Daniel You have no authority, no right to –

Fiona Didn't you hear what he said? That's it. I can't believe that's it.

Daniel looks at her, shocked, almost as if she were a stranger now.

We won, Daniel. Didn't you hear what he said?

NINE

CONCESSION EXPECTED WITHIN THE HOUR

A street. Declan wears a blue safety jacket with 'Press' written on it. Judy is filming him. His face appears on the screen behind, greatly enlarged.

Declan I should stress there's been no official word yet – however, sources close to the President have revealed that his concession is imminent, with his successor expected to make his first address perhaps even as early as tomorrow morning. Now in order to put this in context, Huw, you have to realise the remarkable turnaround in this election. A vote that was expected, by most commentators, to end up more of a coronation than contest for the incumbent President – that all changed when he failed to deliver a first-round, knockout blow to his opponent, triggering the run-off.

Of course the registration of fifty thousand new voters, mostly from the rural regions, has certainly played its part in what is a slim margin of victory, but a win is a win is a win. (*He stops and thinks, dropping his broadcast voice.*) Sorry, Judy, let me try that again.

Declan clears his throat, refocuses and is back into broadcast mode.

My understanding from a senior Election Observer I've spoken to is that the Observation Team, sent, if you like, to rubber-stamp these elections on behalf of the international community – is ready to clarify that key standards were met and that the election was free and fair.

The question, of course, remains whether the violence of the past few days will recede with a new Head of State or indeed intensify, as the harsh reality of governing this divided country replaces the more moderate, some might say, naive rhetoric of his campaign.

Whatever happens now, no one is denying this country has a long road to travel, but tonight, at least, that journey has begun. (*Dropping his broadcast voice*) . . . And then we cut to the kid with the barrel on his head walking along that road?

Judy Okay, they're ready for us . . . And it's not Huw tonight, it's George.

Declan Well, I'm coming home, George, and I want your fucking job.

Judy On air, in five, four, three, two –

TEN

THREE HOURS AFTER
THE OFFICIAL DECLARATION

A hotel room. Daniel stands and faces forward as a patch of blood slowly spreads across his shirt. He is sweating, with a backpack on. We hear the distant rumble of an explosion, then closer, the sound of exploding fireworks. A half-packed suitcase lies on the bed. Fiona calls out from the bathroom offstage.

Fiona (*off*) Where were you? I waited at the office. I've ordered some breakfast. Just some coffee, but if you're hungry we can call down for something else.

If it would help you to work, I mean, or just if you're hungry. Are you hungry?

Daniel I've walked that route my whole life and it's never taken me more than ten minutes. Today it took two hours. I'm sorry.

Fiona enters. She's changed her clothes and is looking washed and fresh. Then she spots Daniel's bloody shirt and her face immediately changes.

Fiona Oh my God! What happened? Daniel.

Daniel Nothing.

Fiona Someone shot you.

Daniel Of course not.

Fiona takes a step towards him, desperate to help, but Daniel retreats a step.

Fiona What happened? Are you cut? Let me see. Daniel, let me . . . (*Pointing at the blood.*) Let me help you.

Daniel No. It's fine. Let it dry.

Fiona Come here.

Daniel Please don't!

They look at one another for a moment before Daniel moves for a chair and starts to unpack his laptop onto a slim table.

When is the press conference?

Fiona It doesn't matter.

Daniel This afternoon?

Fiona Yes, but it doesn't matter.

Daniel They won't send another translator for the report. Not now, there isn't time. You can't move out there, haven't you seen? People are penned in by plastic shields and black helmets but they keep finding ways to burst out and edge forward. You can't contain that amount of people. It never works.

Fiona Let me help you.

Daniel You need my help to finish this, so you can go home. You have to go, while it's safe. That's the most important thing. May I see it?

Fiona picks up the final report, which Daniel takes from her carefully.

And it's been signed off?

Fiona That's it. It'll be our last word on things. We need it translated and copies made . . . but maybe you should read it first.

Daniel looks down at the report hesitantly, before flipping it open and starting to read it. His eyes bore into it. In the background we hear more fireworks as Fiona sits on the edge of the bed. There is silence for some time, then another explosion, which startles Fiona and brings her to her feet.

Fiona What is that?

Daniel (*still reading and without looking up*) Bottles filled with lighter fluid or gasoline. A rag. You light the rag and throw it. It's kids' stuff. Nothing too heavy-duty yet . . . This is a mistake.

Fiona What?

Daniel It's written here that it was their idea to register more voters. Not your idea, but the Electoral Committee. That's a mistake.

Fiona For clarity it's better to keep us out of the picture.

Daniel It's not a mistake then?

Fiona No.

Daniel It's a lie.

Fiona No.

Daniel But it was your idea.

Fiona Look, you're hurt. Cut. You're bleeding, for God's sake. This is no time to –

Daniel A perfect time.

Fiona They're blowing stuff up outside.

Daniel Perfect time to talk . . . to explain it to me. Why would you write that?

Fiona senses his anger. She tries to reason with him.

Fiona It's all about empowering the internal process.

Daniel What does that mean?

Fiona It means it can't come from us.

Daniel But it did. Were you always planning on this? Or are you trying to absolve yourself now, of what's going on outside?

Fiona No, of course not. It just – it muddies the waters to say we were involved.

Daniel looks at her.

I didn't tell people how to vote. And we got rid of a fucking animal. A man who beat people, who shot at trucks, for crying out loud. He fed placards, wooden placards, to students who opposed him. That man is gone.

When I first came here, when we first met . . . the things you said about this country, I thought you meant them.

Daniel I did. I still do.

Fiona Now you have a new administration. A new start. You wanted that. I take it you heard his speech? Your new President? The words he used? He means them. I thought you understood. I really think your father did –

Daniel I wanted this result, just as much as him.

Fiona Of course you did, any reasonable person –

Daniel But not this way. The simple fact is you only acted because you saw a possibility of winning. That's why you got involved. You registered rural voters.

Fiona Not exclusively.

Daniel But mostly.

Fiona Well, they were the most disenfranchised.

Daniel You knew which way they would swing things. Sixteen thousand votes. That's all he lost by. What you did changed everything.

Fiona You don't know that for sure.

Daniel Neither do you. Don't you see the danger in that? You have no idea what effect you had. You can't quantify it. And now you want to deny it was ever your idea in the first place. Change this report.

Fiona What?

Daniel The words. Change them to reflect the part you played in this. You didn't just observe, Fiona. You did much more than that.

Fiona We got more people voting. We empowered thousands of new voters. We gave them the opportunity to choose. They made their choice. I'm sorry if I don't feel bad about that.

Daniel You should.

Fiona Maybe you should feel grateful.

Daniel Do you have any idea how ugly that sounds?

Fiona I don't mean . . . I just mean you can't do this alone. No country can. The organisation, the discipline of democracy, of everything that comes with that – no one can achieve that alone – from inside a country, I mean. People need our help. But everything that will come in the future –

Daniel WE DON'T NEED YOU TO SAVE US.

Fiona is shocked by Daniel's outburst, just as he is. He gathers himself.

Unless we choose our own path, then what is it worth? I hated my President, but I think I hate your intervention more. No doubt you're a good person, you think of yourself as a good person. But what you've done here is wrong, even though it was with the best intentions. Tell me . . . that you know you did more than just observe.

Fiona It would be easier if what you said were true. If you were right and I was wrong. But I'm not wrong and neither are you. This is just the way things are.

Daniel I don't believe that.

Fiona I'm telling you the truth. Anything I've done –

Daniel Say it. Admit it. To me, at least . . .

Fiona We . . . I . . . empowered a great many –

Daniel There's that word again.

Fiona Yes, all right, that word! But it's true, a good word. I was able to empower those people. I had the authority. I was listened to. What is it that you want from me?

Daniel To take some responsibility. To admit you crossed a line. That, if nothing else.

In the background we hear the squeak of a wheel as Chimma enters with a trolley, covered by a beautiful white cloth. Rattling on top of it is a large, shining silver dome.

Chimma Your breakfast, ma'am. (*Glancing at Daniel, registering the blood.*) For one or for two?

Daniel I'm fine.

Chimma (*she nods and lifts the dome*) Coffee and a complimentary fresh fruit platter, to apologise for the broken windows in the foyer.

Fiona That's fine.

Chimma No strawberries today, I'm afraid, no grapes either, lots of melon. Is that okay?

Fiona It's fine, thank you.

Daniel It looks good.

Chimma (*to Daniel*) Anything for you, sir?

Daniel Cold water.

Chimma Of course.

> *She pours Daniel a glass of water and gives it to him. Daniel drinks it down quickly. Fiona catches Chimma looking at the bloodstained T-shirt.*

Fiona Do you have any bandages?

Chimma Yes, ma'am.

Fiona And antiseptic?

> *Daniel hands the glass back to Chimma and she passes him a napkin which he presses to his chest.*

Chimma What was it? A broken bottle?

Daniel A firework.

> *Chimma seems confused.*

I munye nwo oku, ha amalie ka rocket. [*You light them and they fly up like a rocket.*]

Chimma You're joking?

Daniel Someone was celebrating. It flew straight at me.

Chimma Should I dress it? I used to know how, probably still do.

Daniel It's fine.

Chimma Do you want a new shirt at least?

Daniel No. I want her to have to keep looking at me with this shirt on.

Fiona and Daniel look at each other. Another explosion goes off outside as Chimma withdraws and is gone.

Fiona I thought I would stay. For the funeral.

Daniel No.

Fiona I thought you wanted me to –

Daniel It isn't safe. I'll bury him myself.

Fiona I did this for you.

Daniel You did this for yourself. What you've sacrificed to be here . . . this job you put above everything else, it doesn't give you a licence to act this way.
Look outside, Fiona. Time for you to go home, to your husband.

Fiona stops and looks at Daniel. They have parted ways entirely now.

Fiona Yes, I intervened. Yes, I didn't just observe. Is that what you want me to say? I participated . . .

Daniel (*genuine*) Thank you.

Fiona But after everything we've seen –

Daniel It doesn't matter. You shouldn't have done this.

Fiona But if things had stayed the same. If nothing had changed. Would you really still believe that?

Daniel Yes, and so should you.

ELEVEN

PRESS CONFERENCE:
INTERNATIONAL OBSERVER TEAM
PRESENT FINAL ELECTION REPORT

Fiona is standing alone when Judy steps forward from the shadows with a radio mic in her hand. She clips it onto Fiona without her really noticing.

Judy Is it all right like that?

Fiona looks at the mic and then at Judy before she nods. Judy smiles.

About two minutes then? We're just letting the press in. It's packed. Is there anything you need?

Fiona I don't think so.

Judy exits. Fiona looks down at the mic on her lapel and fiddles with it.
    Saunders enters. He has an ID badge around his neck, a mic clipped on and a foam cup of coffee in his hand. He's made more of an effort with his dress today. Fiona doesn't spot him at first.

Saunders If you just talk normally . . . at normal volume, it should pick it up. The mic. They're quite sensitive. I'm going to introduce you, if that's okay. I'm Roger Saunders. From the Embassy.

He holds out his hand. Fiona shakes it. She smiles and looks at her notes.

Nervous?

Fiona Yes.

Saunders Good. They say that's good, don't they? Actors?

Fiona I don't know.

Saunders takes a sip of coffee.

Saunders It's filling up in there. Are you ready to have your photo taken? You look ready. Who would have thought they'd be interested?

Fiona Who?

Saunders You know, people. The wider world. Astonishing. All for this little place. It's all right, I can call it that – I've been here three years.

This interests Fiona. She nods and looks at him for the first time.

Fiona And you're staying?

Saunders Yes, this is my home. Although I go where they send me. A little like you.

Fiona You know local people?

Saunders I have local friends.

Fiona How do they feel about things?

Saunders What things?

Fiona How do they feel about the election, I mean?

Saunders Are you looking for affirmation?

Fiona Sorry?

Saunders Over the moon. Really pleased. Delivered. Is that what you want me to say?

Fiona looks at Saunders, confused.

Fiona I . . .? Do we know each other?

Saunders Yes. No. Well, I've been following you, so strictly speaking, no. I've also been reading your emails, but I think you suspected someone was, because you stopped. You stopped emailing, anything interesting anyway, and your phone calls, too, were a little more sporadic.

Fiona keeps looking at him without speaking. Saunders looks a little embarrassed.

We could have stopped you. At any point. That's probably the first thing I should say. To begin with I had no idea what you were doing . . . although we had our suspicions. Experience teaches you –

Fiona What do you mean? What do you mean, 'we'? How long have you been watching me?

Saunders Since the beginning. Truth is I had my doubts, but when we realised what you were up to people were . . . surprised. Grateful. Very grateful even.

Fiona Which people?

Saunders My people. Your people, Fiona.

Fiona looks disgusted as this slowly sinks in.

Fiona I wasn't . . . I wasn't up to anything.

Saunders The BBC broke the story about the President's concession, seemingly before anyone else even knew. Hours before. Citing a senior Election Observer. Forced the administration to make a statement. Are you telling me you weren't behind that?

Fiona tries to shrug this off, but Saunders keeps looking at her.

Mine is a watching brief. Like yours. I've been in this region three years – waiting. Then you come along and change things in a short space of time. It's impressive. This isn't a game we play much any more. Taking sides, I mean. With the best will in the world, I don't think we'd have been as efficient as you.

Fiona I just did my job.

Saunders Don't be so modest. You did much more than that.

Judy re-enters quickly.

Judy Both all right? There's water out there. Ready when you are.

Judy disappears again. Saunders straightens his tie.

Saunders I spoke to your translator. Nice fellow, Daniel? Don't worry, he didn't say a word against you. Too smart for that, too loyal perhaps. But what I mean is, just think of the good you've done him, his generation.

Fiona I didn't intend . . . Please don't talk like we're on the same side of this.

Saunders But we are. Very much the same side. Don't be so naive, Fiona. Your reasons –

Fiona Our reasons, I'm sure, are very different.

Saunders Are they? Are they really, though? Or does it help you to think that they are? Look, nobody likes violence. You were just trying to do the right thing.

And now here we are. With a little teething trouble on the streets but with a result. The right result. You've helped open this country up, Fiona. Now it can get moving again. Not in five years, not in ten years. Right now. It's what people wanted, and you responded. Sincerely. And now we can play our part in that too. Help them, trade with them, stabilise them. They ought to thank you for what you've done. They ought to but they won't.

Fiona looks at him, horrified.

Of course you may prefer to see it differently. As an accident. You might prefer to go home. To Michael . . . And put all this down to experience – what happened, I mean. But you have to know it's not an accident if you'd do it again.

Fiona stares at him. Saunders waits for her to speak, but she doesn't.

You won't realise the part you've played here for years yet. And I mean in a good way. Up close, from the ground, is not necessarily the best vantage point. Go home. It'll all make more sense from a distance. I'd better go and introduce you.

Fiona watches as Saunders leaves. In these few moments she looks at the report in her hands and seems close to collapse.
Suddenly over a PA we hear Saunders addressing a news conference.

Saunders (*off*) Thank you, everyone. A few bits of housekeeping before we begin . . . This International Observation Mission would not have been possible without a truly international financial effort, so it falls to me to thank the United Nations, the United States Agency for International Development, the European Commission, the Republic of Germany and a number of individual contributors. So that's that bit . . .

Fiona takes a step back, and looks as if she is about to run.

We'll do questions afterwards, let's just hear the statement in full and then, as I say, we'll do any, any questions that you might have after. So, therefore, it gives me great pleasure to introduce the Deputy Chief of the International Election Observation Mission, Fiona Russell to take it from here . . . Fiona?

For a few, agonising moments Fiona still considers disappearing before her face seems to resolve itself. She opens the Final Statement, takes a breath and then looks straight at us.

TWELVE

Fiona remains onstage in a slowly dimming light as Saunders re-emerges.

Saunders She delivered the statement. Of course she did. It was a little shaky, perhaps, but word for word. She answered questions politely. 'The process had been a success. The President had shown great respect for the will of his people. The opposition had fought a spirited campaign.' Clichés, liftable from almost any statement of its kind, but appropriate for a country that has become a part of the real world now. A participant in the grand scheme of things.

She boarded a plane for Heathrow and left. No blue plaque in her hotel room. No hospital named after her. Just gone, suddenly.

Fiona has disappeared into darkness now.

I would like to stay. If that's acceptable. I know, strictly speaking, that it is no longer a small operation. I know you'll want to establish more of a presence here. I'm certain that my broom cupboard will no longer suffice and that a few scratchy emails from me is hardly the way forward. It's a different enterprise now. An outpost no longer . . . but I'd like to stay. In some capacity. If possible. I'll leave it with you.

In terms of shopping . . . I miss cheese with a rind. That's all. See what you can do. Sincerely, Saunders.

The End.